Storied Lives

Discovering and Deepening Your Personal Myth

Craig Chalquist, PhD
with Rebecca Elliott, MA

Book One of the *Living Myth Series*

World Soul Books
654 Center Street
Walnut Creek, CA 94595

Printed in the United States of America
ISBN 9780615270388

Cover photograph by Susan Mills (www.susanmills.net).

Cover design by Rebecca Elliott and Craig Chalquist.

Visit the author's web site at Chalquist.com.

Table of Contents

The Living Myth Series

It has been claimed that we live in a time without myth. But if C.G. Jung, Joseph Campbell, Hermann Hesse, Thomas Mann, Mary Shelley, Robert Graves, Jorge Luis Borges, F. Scott Momaday, and a host of other preeminent minds are correct, then myth is always with us and all around us as the basic psychic weave that holds our relations with ourselves, each other, and the living world. The real question is whether we resonate to the weave of myth consciously or unconsciously, knowingly or involuntarily, even tragically.

The Living Myth Series seeks to foster consciousness of the presence and power of myth in our lives. In the end myth is story, and story always says more about the heights and depths of human experience than facts or figures can by themselves.

The Series is being published at a time when the humanities have yet again been deprived of public funding for being insufficiently "practical." Yet if we knew our stories and traditions better, and valued the richness of our literary and artistic legacies, we might treat each other and the planet itself with greater understanding and compassion. At its best, the study of myth requires imaginative engagement, thinking in the round, intensive self-questioning, and growth of a capacity for grasping contrasting "pantheons" of choices, possibilities, and perspectives. It expands the heart as well as the mind. An education of the soul reaching into multiple levels of the naturally relational self is what this Series hopes to encourage.

ACKNOWLEDGMENTS

The people who made this book possible include Professor Christine Downing, who taught me how specific a personal myth can be; the former students and seminar participants who wrote up their poignant and compelling stories for use herein; John Mabry, who gave me some valuable typesetting lessons; and the School of Holistic Studies at John F. Kennedy University, where I teach a graduate class on Archetypal Mythology. I also extend a special thanks to Rebecca Elliott for help with this book and the blessing of her thoughtfully written chapter.

DEDICATION

To the unsilent gods of my ancestors.

Introduction to the Storied Self

Am I the only one who is confused? I wondered as I sat in class. After all, it was only high school psychology. I understood the theories all right, but shouldn't I be able to meld them into a coherent picture of the self?

Evidently one of my classmates wasn't able to either. After half a semester of seething frustration, he appeared to have a revelation during a discussion of Freud. Pointing his finger directly at the psychology teacher, he declared, "You have a death wish against me!" This was too much for her. She fled the room, and we ended up finishing the semester with a substitute. Spectacular, the power of wit against what Brazilian educator Paulo Freire had named the banker model of education: deposits dumped straight into the heads of passive, disenchanted students. Eventually I lit the school on fire.

This, my first exposure to psychology, was also my first exposure to a field that simultaneously fascinated me even as it turned me against my perceptions. Not until working on my third degree in psychology did I fully grasp the source of my puzzlement: mainstream psychology's abdication of the essence, the meaning matrix, the *story* of persons in favor of describing "the mind" from the "objective" view outside. Gradually I came to see this mechanistic approach as an alienated view of human nature, a nature rendered unnatural because not engaged in except intellectually.

Even in the "hard" sciences a sack of cold data is not an explanation. When you or I ask *why* something is, we aren't looking for only the facts that actually make up the *what*. We are looking for the inside story, the narrative, the tale of what the facts really mean. Without that story-web of connections they mean very little by themselves. A man in a restaurant suddenly explodes at a cashier he wrongly believes to have short-changed him. The outburst surprises everyone, perhaps even him. What are the facts? The volume of his shout, the timing of it, the racing pulses of those within earshot; but unless you know that he just learned his wife was having an affair with his accountant, the incident would remain a mystery no matter how much data you compiled. You wouldn't understand it unless you sat down with him and asked for his point of view.

In retrospect I wish the high school vice principal had asked me why I started the fire. He had some facts too: a good student, if one of the "quiet ones" you have to watch; introspective, shy, clean record. He did not know, of course, that a bully had been beating the tar out of my friends as well as threatening me. He did not ask, either, and so he never realized that it was the bully's locker I lit on fire. The police arrived in time to put it out, but not in time to stop me from knocking out the bully at lunch.

Continuation school offered no psychology courses, but the library contained some of Conan Doyle's Sherlock Holmes novels. I was impressed enough by Holmes's ability to grasp the stories of clients and criminals alike that I read the entire Holmes opus. I did not know it at the time, but I was getting a feel for the exploration of personal stories, and therefore of personal myths. (I later learned to my delight that Freud had been a Holmes fan. No wonder his case histories read like detective stories.)

By contrast, most mainstream psychology books read like heaps of still frames disconnected from the film they are supposed to animate. We read about drives and needs, systems and step functions, instinct and eros, stimulus and response; about cognitive schemata, tests and traits, elaborate evolutionary modules; but where is the living person in all this? Making a similar point, existentially oriented therapists like Rollo May and Irvin Yalom have insisted that we learn little of consequence until we capture hints of a person's inner story from active encounters with it. C. G. Jung, who knew this psychological truth, added a layer of meaning to it by showing how personal stories so often link up with collective ones, with your tale carried within the grand tales—the mythologies—of your time.

Mythologies? Aren't the sciences more precise?

Jung didn't think so. For describing the outward nature of something relatively measurable, science has performed wonders and continues to do so. But to get at the story of a person's life, myth (Jung believed) was a more useful tool. For myth is not an archaic explanation for weather. This Enlightenment-era prejudice was spread around by thinkers afraid of the messy transformative power of a good deep story. Still earlier, this fear had surfaced as *euhemerism*, the idea that myths refer mainly to actual people or events. This idea was started by Euhemeros, a traveler who noticed how Alexander the Great acquired the status of a god once the conqueror had died. Euhemeros failed to notice that the myth was not reducible to the person it had come to surround.

Whereas fact can serve to categorize and compartmentalize dangerously stirring truths, myth is a collectively shaped way to make sense of one's place in the world. The question is not whether we have a mythology or not—everyone does, even rationalists for whom the Big Bang serves as a creation story. The question is whether the mythology still works or has become outdated, devalued, or unconscious.

In India a girl with four arms was born in a destitute village near Bangalore. She was promptly named Lakshmi after the four-armed goddess of beauty, love, and abundance. For non-Indians such an event might seem a random accident of genetics or circumstances, but it made sense to the villagers because they possessed a conscious, working mythology with which to find a meaning in things. Lakshmi is similar in some ways to the Roman Venus (Aphrodite to the Greeks), a loving goddess of inner and outer wealth. As understood through the lens of mythology, the gods had sent a message of comfort through this girl's uncanny birth. To locals this signal of divine light in the darkness of poverty made all the more sense for the birth having taken place on the very day devoted to the celebration of generous Lakshmi.

However revered, mythological systems do get worn out over time, as anyone suspects who has sought refuge in traditional spiritual symbols and creeds only to find them devoid of meaning or feeling. For most of us the ancient names of Zeus and Hera evoke no particular emotion. One could think of an aging religion, to take one example of wear and tear, as a mythology that forgets it is one as it hardens from its original vitality and radicalism into dull literalisms and mindless rules that epitomize what it originally protested. When I worked as a therapist I often met clients who felt crushing guilt over the fact that, bled of all his Dionysian joy and splendor, Jesus meant nothing to them anymore, and no amount of frantic doubt-concealing fundamentalism would restore his name to life in their soul once the spirit had left the letter behind for good. I could sympathize: having been raised in a conservative branch of Lutheranism, I had felt pangs of guilt and envy as a teenager when my praying friends would rapturously call out, "My Lord, my Lord!" With hormones in full motion, all I could think in my sorrow was that if only Jesus had legs like Tina Turner or eyes like Candice Bergen, I could get on board with it all. No such luck. I respected Jesus as great teacher and divine prophet, but as an object of worship his upturned bearded face and punctured arms left my heart and my instincts uninterested.

A myth when alive bridges one's personal story to dimensions of experience that reach beyond the personal. A myth is a story of how people like you and me have encountered the sacred currents of the world washing up all around. Myths personify these currents, give them faces and characters through oral tellings and enacted images and rituals. For the Greeks a moment of exquisite personal power possessed a Zeus or Hera quality, just as a foul-up in communication seemed to exude the sudden presence of tricky Hermes: gods not as nouns or beings to believe in, but as deeply felt characteristics of life welling up over itself like new wine from sturdy bottles.

We might even find that the "mythlessness" upon which our supposedly rational culture insists exhibits an unacknowledged mythic structure. The fantasy of objectivity always brings to mind the famous innkeeper Procrustes, who whacked off the legs of his guests to fit his short bed.

It's possible to study oneself well, be in a lot of therapy, meditate daily, and stay physically and mentally fit, but until we know what myth we live, we remain somewhat illiterate, as though confronted by a pile of books written about ourselves by some unknown author. Being born into a culture blind to myth is a bit like being adopted into a family whose stories cannot explain the lifelong sense of differentness you feel. Why am I like this and not that? Why can't I belong? Why are my passions, my dreams, my likes and dislikes so unlike everyone else's? In such a setting you must do extra work to recover your missing roots.

JUNG'S WORK WITH STORY AND MYTH has spawned quite a few later efforts to track down personal myths. Although useful and educational, most of the guidance provided for these attempts has dealt with archetypes and not myths. An archetype is a general, universal pattern of experience: examples include The Hero, The Divine Child, Love, Beauty, the Sacred Marriage, Transformation, Death, Apocalypse, Initiation Birth, Rebirth. These collective motifs showing up in all times and places are like vessels of potentiality waiting to be filled in with the images and experiences of particular individuals and cultures. That's where the specificity of myth comes in, or should. Lakshmi is not an archetype, just as there is no Hera or Athena or Artemis or Zeus archetype. Lakshmi is a mythic figure who expresses the archetypal Love Goddess. In Greek myth she would look like Aphrodite, in Chinese like Kwan Yin, in Celtic like Deirdre or Aine, in Norse like lovely Freya, builder of bridges and bringer of peace through erotic diplomacy. Archetypes tend to be more general, the factors behind how we see and sense, whereas myths get specific and color them in.

As we will see, one's personal myth reflects that specificity. We can be much more detailed in tracking and discovering the mythic level of ourselves than in settling for archetypal abstractions like Queen, Goddess, King, or Warrior. We can see the ancient stories reinventing themselves in our lives, forever dreaming their myths onward, as Jung so poetically expressed it. Stories live to be retold, not just told over: one reason they grow with the telling.

Besides emphasizing the ever-present specificity of myth lining our lives, another goal of this book is to counter the sales-oriented rush to trade in old for new. The overriding emphasis in personal myth work until now has been on studying one's current myth in order to replace it with a new one. It's as though someone got ahold of Shakespeare's plays and decided out of discomfort to rewrite Iago as a good guy or rescue Duke Senior from the forest. Instead of submitting to mythic plastic surgery, why not explore what is up for us now in greater detail, including the urge to get away from it? Why not open the myth up and let it breathe instead of applying formulae for happy living to it? The alchemists used to insist that the treasure hard to obtain hid down in the dark places, or as Jung would put it, in our complexes. Personal myth work is a chance to stay with and dig into the story deeply enough to find the precious jewel contained within it. As Joseph Campbell pointed out, the gargoyles are there to test the initiant. Running away from them shows an unreadiness to take the deep journey.

In the following pages you will find tools for self-discovery as well as many examples of storied lives. The tools evolved primarily from my training as a depth psychologist, my Archetypal Mythology class at John F. Kennedy University, and a personal myth seminar I conducted over several months. If you have no sense yet of what your myth is or could be, you stand at the beginning of an adventure leading into unexpected depths. Passing through deserts of reductionism and dead ends of cynicism, the patient seeker of motifs, portents, and hints emerges at last into verdant landscapes fertile with the fruits of transformative insights into how very much more there is to a life than we are led to believe.

CHAPTER 1

What Is a Personal Myth?

"I am Oedipus."

When Freud confessed this to his then-friend Wilhelm Fleiss in 1897, he explicitly linked an interest in myth to the intricacies of depth psychology: the kind of psychology that focuses on the unconscious dimensions of psychic life. So stated Dr. Christine Downing, author of *The Goddess*, in a class she taught at Pacifica Graduate Institute. Dr. Downing understood from the inside what it felt like to live within the myth of Persephone, innocently plucking at a flower only to be dragged one day straight down into Hades.

Before taking her class I had read Jung's and Aniela Jaffe's *Memories, Dreams, Reflections*, in which Jung writes of the need to tell his "personal myth," with no real idea of how specific that myth could be. Nor did Freud fully grasp his own declaration, it would seem; he clearly empathized with the old blind king, but in truth he identified with him all the way down to being led into exile by his daughter Anna, as Oedipus had been by Antigone. Freud was disturbed by dreams of injecting patients with poison, and Oedipus by troubled concerns about the plague of Thebes. Neither could accept that the blight originated from within.

As for Jung, he was moving all his life within the story of the German alchemist Faust, with the *shadow* (an archetypal figure which Jung painted as a sinister man in black) standing in for the devilish tempter Mephistopheles, former patient Sabina Spielrein as the tragic lover Gretchen, and the collective unconscious as the mysterious underworld realm of The Mothers. "Two souls have I, alas, within my breast!" The ancient Greeks would have recognized Faust as Prometheus, a Titan god chained to a mountain for a time for brashly giving celestial fire to humanity. Jung had written about being chained to the Caucasus of the unconscious he confronted.

Each of us comes with many sides to our character, many roles, selves, and parts to play depending on time and phase of life. The mythic self is one of them. But it remains invisible until we gain or regain the capacity for thinking and perceiving symbolically.

Symbolic and Mythic Knowing

Back in the mid-1800s, French medical student Pierre Janet made a crucial discovery in the mental hospital where he worked. He discovered that psychological symptoms could serve as reenactments of wounds never spoken about and therefore never healed.

Janet was an altogether remarkable researcher. He coined the word "subconscious" after a patient told him, "I cry and I do not know why." How could she not know why? Through a "narrowing of consciousness" which we now think of as repression, and through "redoublement," the splitting and dissociation of consciousness so often seen in lingering trauma. Janet took thorough case histories, noted the *rapport magnétique* or "somnambulic influence" of therapist over patient (the transference), moved away from his mentor Charcot's emphasis on hereditary factors even as Charcot still fed his patients iron pellets, theorized that "fixed ideas" (later called "complexes" by Jung) kept old wounds from healing, asked patients to overcome internal censorship by writing down quickly whatever came to mind (free association), and assembled a system of diagnosis and treatment to trace symptoms and fixations to their psychic depths ("profoundeur"). Janet called all this "psychological analysis," a term echoed in 1896 in the name "psychoanalysis" after ambitious Freud had been to France and returned to Vienna eager to put his own system together.

As Janet had learned, unconscious forces do not simply vanish. They reappear in symbolic reenactments, as when a woman whose brother drowned marries a man who also drowns. We constantly and unconsciously enter into and even recreate unfinished dramas, not because we are naturally self-destructive (as Freud had thought), but to give ourselves a chance to heal from the original trauma by making the story come out differently.

The deep psyche speaks most naturally in symbols. The currents and eddies of depths which Freud correctly called "primary" precede and animate the ego world of linear expression and logic. This language of symbols appears not only in symptoms but in dreams, in Freudian slips, in certain kinds of purposeful forgetfulness, in fantasy, in literature and film and art—and in myth.

Myth is metaphoric, as mythologist Joseph Campbell often pointed out. In some ways myth is to a culture what dream is to an individual: tellings from underneath the surface of daily consciousness. Myth carries forward collective visions of the hopes and battles that make life worthwhile. Less contrived than allegory, myth is a brew of worldview, group dream, group bias, inner wisdom, norm, value, and narrative.

In myth appear the basic structures of consciousness given cultural form: assertive Athena wisdom, boundless Kuan Yin kindness, dangerous Frost Giant ego inflations, redemptive Osiris returns of the light. Through its stories shine figurations of the deepest dimensions of human experience, with the chaotic, the nonhuman, the exquisitely human, and the sacred all alchemized and crystallized into oral tellings washed down through time.

"Personal myth" sounds self-contradictory until we understand myth to be a primal language of the soul. To have a personal myth is to be located within a historic tradition, to be woven into a collective fabric of image and sense. It is to find oneself joined directly to the fundamental questions of being human:

Why am I here? Why do things matter? Where did I come from, and where am I going? How do I get there?

Personal Mythologizing: A Quick Survey of the Literature

Jung had discussed the need to know one's myth and to live it as far back as 1952, when he wrote the preface to the fourth edition of *Symbols of Transformation.* Not until later in his life, however, did he discern the figure of Faust standing behind him.

In 1956 psychoanalyst Ernst Kris used the term "personal myth" in the title of a paper to refer to a fantasized or idealized story about one's past. For decades Alfred Adler had been maintaining that a person's "style of life" constituted a kind of working fiction or fantasy system for organizing goals and the sense of self. Neither Adler nor Kris held personal myth as anything beyond the personal, however, a narrowing of focus held to by psychologist Dan MacAdams in *The Stories We Live By* (1993).

By 1961 Jung had published the quasi-autobiography *Memories, Dreams, Reflections* ("quasi" because Aniela Jaffe wrote some of it and heavily edited the manuscript) to explore his myth, although he did not identify it explicitly there as Faust. In 1965 psychology professor Art Warmoth, having worked with Abraham Maslow, wrote about peak experiences and mystical encounters as a kind of substitute mythology in which direct experience assumes the role of what was formerly collective symbolism. (Both humanistic and transpersonal psychology have tended to emphasize individual experience over communally negotiated reality.)

Inspired by the work of Jung, Joseph Campbell began lecturing on personal myth in 1972 and continued on into 1973; some of his lectures appear in the chapter on "Personal Myth" in his book *Pathways to Bliss.* Campbell too discussed myth in terms of general patterns rather than the reliving of specific stories.

When philosopher and men's movement figure Sam Keen began writing and lecturing on personal myth during these years—see *Your Mythic Journey* with Anne Valley-Fox—he went so far as to say that one could actually change one's myth. To some this came as a great relief. Many people feel a heavy reluctance to embrace their myth, especially when it intertwines with early psychological wounding. Some regard it as a threat to their sense of autonomy, like Neo in the *Matrix* films being unwilling at first to recognize himself as a redeemer figure because he wanted to feel in charge of his life. In any case by "personal mythology" Keen meant the collection of stories we use to make sense of ourselves to ourselves. For him personal myth work meant self-exploration through storytelling.

In 1979 and again in 1989, psychologist Stanley Krippner organized symposia to bring a humanistic perspective to personal myth work and vice versa. One result was the book *Personal Mythology* (1988) by Krippner and psychologist David Feinstein, revised in 1997 into *The Mythic Path.* According to Feinstein, a personal myth involves the ongoing construction of inner reality, a project with very concrete outer consequences. For example, from inside the story we draw toward us the people and scenes that serve it, mostly without realizing what we are doing until we find out what the story is. From the start, however, Feinstein's emphasis is on transforming the myth into something else. For humanistic psychology, personal myth work constitutes an individual passageway toward psychic wholeness. Observing this warily, Jungian analyst James Hillman would ask throughout his own work: What do the myths and the images want? To be "integrated," or to be respected on their own imaginal terms as valid entities in and of themselves?

In 1981 Christine Downing published *The Goddess*, and by doing so gave the discussion of personal myth a deepening that would carry myth work well beyond the building deluge of self-help and pop psychology. Eschewing the chance to offer a typology of deities to try on (viz. Jean Shinoda Bolen's often-praised *Goddesses in Everywoman* published in 1984, to be followed five years later by *Gods in Everyman*), Downing told their stories in a way that connected them intimately to women's experience while respecting their status and reality as archetypal presences.

1990 saw publication of Campbell biographer Stephen Larsen's *The Mythic Imagination.* Although Larsen emphasized constructing a personal myth ("conscious mythmaking") more than uncovering one, he too was aware of the possibility of being unconsciously possessed by the power of an unworked myth: an especially large risk in a culture blind to myth and to the subjective in general. Rollo May had pointed out the dangers of this blindness—widespread meaninglessness, inner emptiness, seizure by isms, worship of authority—in his final book, *The Cry for Myth*, published in 1991.

In 1993, the year McAdams published *The Stories We Live By*, Jungian psychotherapist D. Stephenson Bond came out with *Living Myth: Personal Meaning as a Way of Life*. For him, a living myth keeps us related to our surroundings on the one hand and to the psyche on the other while countering the widespread sense of our lives as plotless and meaningless, a direct result of the breakdown of our culture's formerly working myths. However, Bond believes personal myths to be uncommon and sporadically encountered rather than something everyone arrives in life surrounded by.

James Hillman understood this differently. All this time he had been harboring a more or less private view—the "acorn theory"—he had shared with a few friends but no one else. In 1996 he came out with it in the New York Times bestseller *The Soul's Code: In Search of Character and Calling*. "Each person enters the world called," he declared, called by the soul or daimon or "acorn" of the vocational oak tree we are meant to grow. Doing what he refers to as reading biography backwards, his book provides many fascinating examples of how the inklings of their calling appeared early on in the lives of famous people. Think about Winston Churchill and his childhood stuttering. Mainstream psychology would read his later public career reductively, as a form of compensation; by contrast Hillman argues: Of course he stuttered! Something deep within him already knew he'd save England by the power of his voice one day. Or take young Yehudi Menuhin smashing a toy violin—not out of an uncharacteristic petulance, but because his daimon, the calling he came in with, knew even in childhood that it required the real instrument.

Just who, mythologically speaking, is the bearer of the calling? How do myths move from being collective stories floating in the cultural unconscious down into the realm of the personal?

Your Mythic Self

Your personal myth is the collectively storied aspect of who you deeply are.

It would be equally valid to say, however, that you are an aspect of it. Your personal myth images your transhuman side in storied form, and you live within that story as it unfolds. Personal myth is the story you are inside of and that bears on your sense of yourself, your relationships, your occupation, your vocation, and your place in the world.

And so another question: Is one's personal myth created or uncovered? Do we make it or discover it?

It is possible to hold personal myth either way: as a working fiction for making sense of a life, or as fabled role and destination toward which we gradually walk. As something we come in with, our myth shows up in our names, the circumstances of our birth, the place we grew up in, the family constellation we are familiar with. Whatever its ultimate origin, our myth remains open to—and even yearns for—creative elaboration.

Be elaborated it must, for as depth psychology has taught us over a century of psychotherapy and cultural analysis, what we ignore and deny in ourselves eventually returns to haunt us as a rigidly literalized replay of the same old tale, its victim a weary Sisyphus forever pushing his rock uphill and forever watching it tumble down.

When Freud began telling the public about the unconscious, many shuddered and took refuge in quick mind cures. A similar fear lurks behind the popular and cheerful idea that when we are living a "wrong myth" we can change it into a better one, rather like putting on a more fashionable garment or changing one's European name to that of a Hindu saint. As though you could change your ethnicity, natal chart, or DNA. The underlying impulse seems to be a rush to find a more comfortable self instead of really getting to know the current one's disturbing intricacies.

Furthermore, most cases of having a "wrong myth," perhaps every case, turn out upon closer inspection to be a constrictive overidentification with one of the current myth's cast of characters. Feinstein offers the example of Scrooge, whose materialistic mythology wasn't serving him. From this book's point of view it served him marvelously because the whole point of the Scrooge tale is the motif of redemption. Without his nighttime conversion the tale would have been pointless. The determination with which Scrooge clings to his selfishness brings to light one source of the widespread poverty which Dickens wrote to protest. It is fortunate indeed that no one told Scrooge to revision or transform his myth until it was ready to do so on its own.

Little wonder so many of us carry an unconscious fear of even discovering our myth. What Arthur wants to be betrayed by Guinevere again or witness another fall of Camelot? Would you choose the lethal, unrequited love of a Lady of Shallot? What playful Coyote wants to be smashed by the rolling rock in an old Navajo tale? At bottom this is the same fear as that of accessing an old sorrow or an old anger or hurt: What if it takes me over?

Consciousness makes all the difference. We run a far greater risk of being taken over by returns of the repressed, whether personal and "inner" or mythical and collective, when we turn away from confronting them. Not knowing one's myth is the surest way to experience it as fate, as Jung pointed out.

When we confront it, it begins to change. The very act of turning toward some surfacing story or buried complex softens it and transforms it as the story changes *from the inside.* Maybe this time Lancelot will die and Elaine will become first knight. Or neither will die and both will get married, to each other or to someone else. Promethean Jung drank plenty of burgundy in his time, but his liver never gave out, let alone found itself pecked by an eagle or a vulture sent by Zeus. The story's original elements all come into play, but when given a proper welcome, their hard literality softens and gives way to more symbolic replays, more metaphorical stagings.

That welcoming consciousness can also be exercised by the quality of the choices we make within the story. Steinbeck's myth was Lancelot. He knew this partially, but he never knew it entirely. The night before he married a singer named Gwen (!) after having conducted a secret affair with her, he suffered nightmares warning him not to go forward with the marriage. Had he understood this part of his myth better he could have chosen otherwise; but he did marry her, and the marriage turned out to be a disaster for both of them. It nearly always is disastrous when the myth pushes itself forward unconsciously. To be unknowingly identified with a myth is to be its puppet. To understand it deeply is to cut the strings and rewrite the script from within it. The stage remains the same, at least at first, but the plot can turn out differently.

Another common fear of encountering one's myth is the fear of an inflated ego. Abraham Maslow named this the Jonah Complex. Who am I to think I have a Zeus, Hera, or Lakshmi side? How dare Christine Downing think of herself as Persephone? Well, who are any of us to believe we have any direct contact at all with the sacred dimensions of existence? Because that is what a personal myth does, like a tribal mask by which we put on the attributes of the totem, guide, or god who has claimed us. The great mystics and spiritual seers have told us for millennia that, contrary to what religious clerics and their self-preserving institutions maintain, we all come in bearing a precious spark of the divine. The personal myth is the code that unlocks whatever story the divine is manifesting in a life. We could also think of our myth as a sparkling membrane through which the archetypal world and the daytime world flow into each other. The person-shaped distillation they leave behind is what we normally think of as biography.

Personal myth: the biography behind your biography. Your myth could be an ancient one, but its reactivation always says something about the time and place you were born into. For that reason the myth gives you a preset collection of possible directions for personalizing your response to the collective situation.

But do we have only one personal myth?

Nested Myths

For centuries a mythic presence has haunted my homeland. After the conquest of Mexico, a story began to grow about how a lovely young woman named Maria or Laura gave birth to the child or children of her lover, only to be cast aside for another. When he declared that he would take his offspring with him and depart, she was said to have brought them to a lake or river shimmering below a full moon. There she drowned them, calling out, "O my children!" in despair. She lost her mind, and when she finally died, she was destined to wander near bodies of water at night, crying out for the lost little souls until she finally found them. In Mexico she is called La Llorona, the sorrowful, black-garbed Weeping Woman.

Like many old stories, this one has a way of coming back to life when the proper conditions occur. In the Weeping Woman's case those conditions include a recent conquest of territory. As I documented in my book *Deep California*, La Llorona sightings have occurred in all the Mission cities of the Golden State, and she reappears in dream, in artwork, in folklore, etc. whenever new territory is paved down and asphalted over. Andrea Yates, who loved boating and swimming and living near water, was dubbed a modern La Llorona when she drowned her biblically named children in a bathtub in Houston. She was prone to post-partum psychosis that went undiagnosed. Her husband Russell worked for NASA, whose mission remains the "conquest" of space. Set the stage and the myth reawakens, with or without an adequate container.

I was born near San Diego Bay under a full moon. My birth mother did not want to have children, but my father had threatened to leave her unless she did, so she arranged a secret adoption and told my family and my father that I had died at birth of heart failure. According to the adoption paperwork, she suffered one sharp pang of loss and regret at the moment of relinquishment. I do not know if she cried out, "O my child!" but I do know her name, which was Lorna, and the odd fact that she had been born without night vision. Succumbing to Alzheimer's, she lost her mind and died still trapped by her myth. She refused to see me, so we were never reconciled.

For a long time I wondered why I had been born into this myth as a son of Llorona, right down to nearly drowning twice as a child and once as a young adult. My dissertation research showed me a connection between appearances of the archetypal Weeping Woman and the conquests she protests: "archetypal" because she is found around the world, whether her name is Llorona, Crying Wind, Banshee, or Medea. Imagining her tears as those of the wounded landscapes she haunted, I realized that Llorona's story connected me intimately and profoundly to used up, worn out, ecologically devastated California. In fact I had been born on July 6, the day Europeans first spotted the West Coast from the waters off Baja. The myth had shown me my place in depth.

My question was then: What did this myth-rich land want from me?

Llorona had followed the Cross and Sword of the mission-building conquistadors and padres northward from San Diego (the city of my birth) to Sonoma. To understand my ties to coastal California, I spent five years traversing the Mission Trail in the footsteps of the Weeping Woman and Junipero Serra, head of the missionary project in Alta California. As I did this Llorona began to change in my dreams from wailing ghost dressed in black into white-clad mother cradling a child. When I fully understood her to be the imaginal "voice" of the traumatized landscape echoed down into folklore, symptom, art, and dream, my dreams shifted again as I felt myself moving out of the old myth and into a new one. I could feel my spiritual job description change as a result of what I had learned.

The new myth contained elements of the old one, including images of drowning and the core motif of the wandering, displaced son of an abandoned mother and an absent father. It also picked up where the other tale left off. What happens to Llorona's son if he opens his eyes and survives? Well, perhaps the exile is looked after by wise Athena, known to the Romans and the Great Seal of California as armed and armored Minerva. Maybe he spends time living with a hard-to-leave mate in an apartment complex called Capri, the name of the home of the Sirens. Or he spends six years counseling groups of emotionally immature men incarcerated for committing violent crimes. Moving restlessly from Mission county to Mission county, he might even meet his maternal grandfather, described as an "ogre" by the rest of the family, a one-eyed grouch who greeted his long-lost grandson with the words, "By what name should I call you?"

Call me Nobody...

As Homer wrote about Odysseus:

> Sing in me, O Muse, and through me tell the story of that many-sided man who wandered far and wide after sacking the hallowed heights of Troy. Many were the cities he saw and the minds he learned from; and many too the sorrows he suffered, heartsick on the open sea, and fighting to save his life and to bring all his men back home again.

After living in a tool shed in the mountains, presenting my research findings to Pacificans standing in for the friendly Phaeacians, and building a bed for a patiently waiting Penelope, I looked up one morning to see an eagle soaring overhead, thought about Zeus, renounced the vengeful fantasy of organizing enough manpower to kick out the industrially destructive "suitors" of California by force—and felt the myth release me. A lifetime spent feeling like a wanderer in my own homeland was over.

My research had shown me not only how deeply implicated my story was in that of California's, but how to finally feel at home here. For I belonged to this place. With that knowing permeating me, the imaginal hole punched in my unfailed heart by the circumstances of early relinquishment finally closed.

> We feel ourselves to be outsiders, uprooted, in exile here below. We are like Ulysses who had been carried away during his sleep by sailors and woke in a strange land, longing for Ithaca with a longing that rent his soul. Suddenly Athena opened his eyes and he saw that he was in Ithaca. In the same way every man who longs indefatigably for his country, who is distracted from his desire neither by Calypso nor by the Sirens, will one day suddenly find that he is there.
>
> — Simone Weil, *Waiting for God*

Eventually I realized that in my life, the mythic roles of Llorona's son and Ulysses are embraced in turn by an even wider tale. This tale I believe to be lifelong, my mythic bedrock, the storied core of my transpersonal self. It echoes in my name, my ethnicity, and in other lifelong synchronicities. The other myths did not.

It could be, then, that one's true personal myth is there from the start and organizes all later events, encounters, metaphors, subplots, and meanings. It points unerringly forward, incorporates all later temporary stories, and recedes toward the horizon of the future. It is the axis around which a life turns. In some cases it is so obvious that a person recognizes it as soon as it is stumbled upon. In others—mine, for instance—it requires more labor to excavate.

What matters most is to work with whatever myth you find yourself in by discovering it, learning its pitfalls and potentialities, and finding out what it wants by way of elaborative retelling, reflection, and recasting. Only then will it have the psychic space it needs to undergo deep self-transformation.

As the following chapter will show, seeing how this works itself out in a life can be easier to spot when that life is a public one.

CHAPTER 2
Fabled Lives and Public Figures

Figuring out someone's myth is a bit like figuring out one of their dreams: you can't really do it adequately without their help. You see it from the outside; they live it from the inside.

For that reason the following examples should be taken as nothing more than speculative attempts to draw parallels between well-known myths and people's lives. These attempts are snapshots for an exercise in hunting and imagining personal myths: in this case the myths of famous people, stories of their times and souls writ large.

Historical Figures

Sigmund Freud

The story of Oedipus originated as a myth long before Aeschylus turned it into a trilogy of plays in 467 BCE. Only one, the last, survives. The best-known version of the story, and the one which made such an impression on Freud, is the later trilogy written by Sophocles.

Our Oedipus was born into a family that named its sons after kings. Sigisimund himself was treated like a king, even enjoying his own room while the rest of his cramped family made do sharing. He named a younger brother Alexander. A piano whose sounds he found annoying was promptly removed at his complaint.

Both Freud and Oedipus were the focus of prophecies told about their future influence. Oedipus literally married his mother; Freud was highly favored by his—to the extent of being emotionally incested by her—while his father remained a distant but hard-working figure. She called her child "my golden Siggie" even after he urinated on the floor of his parents' bedroom, presumably as a gesture of contempt for his father. In his self-analysis the adult Freud owned up to feelings of intense rivalry, antagonism, and guilt for surpassing the rather unsuccessful male parent.

This Oedipal rivalry played out repeatedly with other men in Freud's professional arena, many of whom he tried to supplant. Having heard of Pierre Janet's work in Paris, Freud rushed back to Vienna to bully physician Josef Breuer into co-publishing a book on the cathartic cure which supposedly originated in Breuer's work with the patient case-named Anna O. Breuer's case notes and letters to other physicians reveal no such cure: no symbolic interpretation of symptoms, no deep digging into the psyche, no insights claimed from unconsciousness. Little wonder Breuer believed the case a total failure, especially when Anna (real name Bertha Pappenheim) continued to languish as a morphine-addicted inpatient until she managed to heal herself many years later. *Studies in Hysteria* having been published, Freud repaid Breuer's fatherly kindness toward him by cutting him off personally and professionally. He also dumped Wilhelm Fleiss after appropriating his theory of childhood sexuality; likewise Jung, who had experimented with complexes, and Adler, who described an early version of the death drive. (Adler's reaction was characteristically jovial: "I make him a present of it!")

Oedipus was traveling by chariot when he encountered the father he would kill. Freud retained a lifelong phobia of trains and rode them only with great reluctance. One of his best-known cases involved analyzing a boy's fear of horses almost entirely through the father. "Little Hans" (the composer Herbert Graf) had seen a horse pulling a cart fall over and kill a bystander. Projecting his myth, Freud believed that part of the boy's trouble involved an unconscious desire to possess his mother and do away with his father.

As a threshold guardian, the Egyptian figure of the Sphinx has been interpreted as an image of psyche itself, particularly in its feminine aspect. The Sphinx ate travelers who could not answer her famous riddle: "What is it that walks on four legs in the morning, on two at noon, and on three in the evening?" "Man," replied Oedipus: for man crawls on all fours, then walks on two, then needs a cane in old age. Upon hearing this, the Sphinx either leaped into an abyss or consumed herself, depending on the tale, and thereby cleared the road to Thebes.

No one familiar with Freud's emphasis on orifices will be surprised that the word "sphinx" goes back to "sphincter." In 1906, Freud's equivalent of admiring Thebans gave him a medallion for his 50th birthday depicting Oedipus solving the riddle of the Sphinx. Replicas of the beast sat behind and overlooked Freud's desk and perched at the foot of the symbolic bed of the analytic couch. Did its bare breasts remind him of his mother and evoke his myth?

He had written of mothers as the "child's first seducer," married a motherly woman who took care of him, and dreamed in childhood of two or three tall, robed people wearing bird beaks while carrying his lifeless mother into the room. Analyzing the dream as an adult, he was reminded of hawk-headed Egyptian funerary gods and of a childhood companion telling him about sex. At some level he would probably have enjoyed seeing that massive and seductive feminine presence unraveled and banished from his cares (had he not dreamed of his wife's favorite flower smashed in a textbook?), but his mouth remained at the nipple of his cigars even after a diagnosis of mouth cancer. He dutifully ate Sunday dinner with his mother even though it always gave him a stomach ache. He must have hated her deeply.

With his mother Jocasta Oedipus fathered four children, two boys and two girls; with Martha, Freud fathered five, but Sophie died of a battlefield infection at the end of World War I, leaving behind two boys and two girls, one of whom was Anna, "my Antigone." Just as Antigone was confronted by the authoritarian Cleon, so Anna was confronted by the SS. As with Oedipus, she led her father into exile (in Freud's case London). As for the sons, those of Oedipus were called "warlike" by Pindar; Freud's two sons had served in the army.

With Sophie lost to the plague of war, Freud set himself to discover the roots of human violence. After much research he wrote about the murder of a prehistoric primal father. Oedipus, also seeking to understand a plague, learned that its sources led to the death of the former king. Oedipus refused to see himself as the killer; Freud turned everyone into a killer and thereby avoided the harder task of uncovering and healing the emotional origins of hostility, origins that included stepping on others to get ahead, self-aggrandizement, fear of insignificance, and repressed hatred. Adrift in self-blindness, Oedipus left Thebes on the arm of Antigone and was placed under protection by the King of Athens. Hounded by the Nazis, Freud left Vienna with Anna, heir to his version of psychoanalysis, with the assistance of the influential Princess Marie Bonaparte.

> Oedipus attempted to apply the abilities of a modern police detective to the task of the reconstruction and clarification of all the events connected with his birth. Instead, he made the acquaintance of the mystery and tragedy that lie behind every human life; the drama tells us quite literally that blindness, rather than clarity, lay at the end of his path.
>
> — Luigi Zoja, "Analysis and Tragedy"
> (*Post-Jungians Today*, p. 38)

Even before his death, Freud's followers were rewriting substantial portions of psychoanalytic history, turning him into the sexual liberator, originator of depth psychology, and teacher of Jung found in so many later texts now under reexamination by subsequent scholarship. Having poured scorn onto religion, the band of brothers now enacted their own, with Freud as its prophet, materialism as its dogma, and Eros and Death as its two-god pantheon.

Nevertheless, kingly Freud is sure to hold his throne in history as a great synthesizer and clarifier of psychological ideas. Having missed his calling, which was archeology (therapy bored him, few if any patients were truly healed, and several of his patients and followers committed suicide), Freud drew fully upon his considerable natural fund of creativity in psychology's early days despite his personal burdens and beasts.

Like no one before him he demonstrated brilliantly and with great clarity the prevalence of unconscious conflict, desire, and defense. He was a man "in the grip of his daimon," as Jung pointed out, which in the end meant in the grip of his myth.

C. G. Jung

Versions of the tale of Faust, the magician who sells his soul to the devil, go back to the Germany of the 1500s and beyond, but the one Jung most identified with and read as a child was Goethe's. Jung liked to think he was a descendant of the famous polymath and playwright.

Goethe's version opens with Mephistopheles betting God that His servant Faust can be turned to evil: an echo of the Old Testament story of Job. As Jung wrote in his book *Answer to Job*, he too would come to see his entire life as one long struggle with the divine. Like Faust, Jung experienced himself as divided into two selves often in opposition. How to unite them without silencing either?

The alchemist Faust sought to discover the spark that animated all life. In this aspiration he took after Prometheus, who created people from clay. Faust's assistant created a homunculus. As a boy, Jung the future psychological alchemist created a small manikin and equipped it with a black river stone for use as a "power source" of what he would later identify as psychic energy. One day he would carve a homunculus in stone. He was also fascinated by corpses: once-living bodies devoid of animation.

After Christianity and positivistic science had both failed to quench Jung's Faustian thirst for knowledge, Mephistopheles appeared to him as an inner figure he identified as the shadow: a personification of what we repress into unconsciousness. The shadow led him into worlds like those seen by Faust shortly before catching up with Helen of Troy and Gretchen, two examples of what Jung would call the anima: the feminine aspect of the male mind and connecting link to Faust's "realm of the Mothers," the collective unconscious.

Gretchen wanted Faust but feared her mother. The mother of former patient Sabina Spielrein wrote Jung an angry letter demanding that he break off his affair with her daughter. Jung's blunt response was no sleeping potion, but the affair eventually ended after Spielrein confessed to Gretchen-like fantasies of being pregnant with Jung's child. Many years later Spielrein would end up in her own sad equivalent of Gretchen's place of execution and be shot in cold blood by the Nazis.

Goethe took decades to finish the second part of *Faust*, which he finally concluded the year he died. It was almost too much for him to work on. So it was with Jung's famous "confrontation with the unconscious" and the tremendous amount of writing that emerged from that fiery series of inner encounters.

Recovering from his own set of otherworldly shocks, Faust won the hand of Helen by dressing up as a knight like those seen in Jung's dreams and visions. Helen eventually returned to the underworld (receded into the unconscious), but Faust's prosperity and reputation continued to increase (as did Jung's). Part of this involved reclaiming land from the sea and building a palace (Jung's Tower) near the shore.

Just here the myth changed significantly, for where Faust had been responsible for the deaths of the old couple Baucis and Philemon, Jung welcomed their imaginal counterparts into his circle of consciousness. Inviting them into his fantasies, he held conversations with them and heeded their advice.

At this point, Jung was fully aware his myth. As he recorded in 1942 in a letter to Paul Schmitt,

> ...All off a sudden with terror it became clear to me that I have taken over Faustas as my heritage, and moreover as the advocate and avenger of Philemon

> and Baucis, who, unlike Faust the superman, are host of the gods in a ruthless and godforsaken age...
>
> — quoted by Sonu Shamdasano, "Who is Jung's Philemon?" (*Jung History*, 2(2), p. 1)

In *Memories, Dreams, Reflections*, Jung's comments show how profoundly he embraced his myth:

> ...When Faust, in his hubris and self-inflation, caused the murder of Philemon and Baucis, I felt guilty, quite as if I myself in the past had helped commit the murder of these the two old people. This strange idea alarmed me, and I regarded it as my responsibility to atone for this crime, or to prevent its repetition.

Before his death, Faust, who had consorted with the Spirit of Nature, fell into a moment of supreme beauty. Jung found his in a coma during which he seemed to see the entire Earth from space: the most wondrous sight of his life. So miraculous was this vision that he had trouble getting interested in life once again after being discharged from the hospital. No doubt his mythic self, having been so often to the underworld (for both Faust and Prometheus are tricksters and psychopomps), yearned to follow the Faustian path straight into heaven and redemption; but Jung's assumption of conscious responsibility for the myth had already changed it, and as psyche's burly spokesman he had more work to do in this world.

Wolfgang Amade Mozart

When the ancient Greeks formed a procession at Athens to participate in the fabled mystery rituals at Eleusis, they were led by a childlike figure bearing a torch. He stood in for Iacchus, son of the grain goddess Demeter, the divine child whose star-like radiance lit the underworld darkness. Some identified him as a boyish variant of the ecstatic god Dionysus, others as a personification of the holy enthusiasm of the rites themselves. The Romans thought of him as

Liber and associated him with masks, togas, and song-making.

Jung had him in mind when he wrote about the *puer*, the mythic eternal boy always accompanied by Old Man *senex* as persistently as authority figures like archbishops and creditors and stern Leopold Mozart pursued the bright boy of music across the great stage that-was and is Vienna. Picture the stony Commendatore condemning the torch-lit libertine Don Giovanni. Ever aloft, filled with ideas, the flying, fleeing, dancing *puer* takes no thought of consequences or practicalities or hard realities until they start to bury him. Picture Michael Jackson, a self-identified Peter Pan always pursued by some relentless Captain Hook.

Mozart's parallel to the Eleusinian Mysteries was Freemasonry. His brilliance shone over the death music he composed for a fellow Mason and sparkled and flashed in the Masonic imagery of many compositions, including The Magic Flute, written down in a rainy shack near the common people's theater while his wife was away recovering her health. So celestial were the songs pouring forth from singing Mozart that Beethoven, hearing them, gave up on composing operas.

The Divine Child wears too many forms to count; in folklore he or she often shows up to lead and advise the bewildered. Sometimes he appears as exuberant Dionysus, of whom Iacchus represents a byform. Candidates for possession by this vine god of ecstacy include such varied personalities as Jim Morrison (who once called himself Dionysus and was surrounded by maenad groupies), Jesus of Nazareth ("I am the vine, you are the branches," turner of water into wine, and pulled apart on the cross, his garments divided), and Nietzsche, who described himself as Dionysus Zagreus shortly before being mentally dismembered by syphilis. The Welsh knew the god as Mabon. Psychotherapists put on the mask of Dionysus when therapy enters into cathartic drama.

Joan of Arc

The armor, the sword, the victorious battlefield wisdom, the inner illumination, the chastity motif: in these facets of the Maid of Orleans we can recognize She whom the Greeks knew as Athena and the Romans as Minerva, armored goddess of polis and culture sprung one bright day from the head of Zeus.

Joan's leadership—that of a white-armored adolescent on horseback—carried forward a series of attacks that reversed the progress of the Hundred Years War in favor of badly beaten France. From one battle she came away with an arrow wound to the neck; from another, with a crossbow puncture in her leg; from yet another, with a helmet dented from a cannonball. She was captured by the English during a fight in 1430 only because she insisted on being the last to retreat.

She was burned not just once, but thrice at a stake in Rouen on a trumped-up charge of heresy. This circle of illumination, fiery from her visions of the saints and lethal from the coals at her feet, extends to her mythic sisters St. Brigid, whose flame is kept lit at Kildare in Ireland, White Buffalo Calf Woman, who came to the Sioux surrounded by light, and Kali, byform of Durga, wielder of swords and slayer of demons. Even gentle Sophia, who upbraided the boastful Demiurge in Gnostic lore, possesses a touch of the assertiveness that always emanates from the goddesses of wisdom. Although sometimes mistaken as goddess of war, more often they are builders of culture, bestowers of tools, and bringers of craft and education. They appear when the people they favor feel the desperation of the lost, bewildered, and defeated.

Sir Isaac Newton

As Meynard Keynes observed, Newton was not the first of the age of reason so much as the last of those who saw the universe as magical in the way of the Babylonians and Sumerians. Born prematurely in 1642 on Christmas Day by the old calendar and January 4th by the new, his Janus propensity for being a liminal figure, one face looking forward and the other backward, has been noted by B. J. T. Dobbs and other Newton scholars. The Roman god of beginnings, portals, passageways, and endings and who gave his name to January has been depicted holding a key and wearing the sun and moon for faces: alchemical symbols which Newton, an alchemist from 1669 to 1696, knew well. As a young child he had written in his notebooks from both ends at once and left his name carved on windowsills.

Newton's later-life job as master of the mint (where he transitioned the national standard from silver to gold) echoed Janus's role as guardian of money. Whereas Janus had allied himself to Saturn and by doing so inaugurated a Golden Age, Newton marked the climax of both the Scientific Revolution and the Renaissance.

He had sought the hinge between the worlds of spirit and matter, the ethereal and the material, a clockwork vision of the cosmos never having satisfied him. He died in old age while having abdominal cramps: an onset of metaphoric labor pains as antiquity gave birth to modernity.

Harry Houdini

Houdini: so slippery that he even Americanized his birthplace despite being born in Hungary. Houdini was not his real name. The man born Erich Weiss got it from another famous magician after debuting on the trapeze as "Prince of the Air" at age 10.

Escapes were Houdini's ultimate trickster specialty. He got out of ropes, chains, boxes, handcuffs, straitjackets, police vans, mailbags, and even tanks filled with water. He also pretended to be a medium on occasion and enjoyed debunking spiritualists with their own eye-fooling methods. Hermes, called Mercury by the Romans, would have laughed at this, for the god of messages also managed communication between the living and the dead. (One of Houdini's acts was called Buried Alive.)

Nor would it have surprised the shapeshifting god of commerce, thievery, and fast transportation that Houdini taught himself to drive and fly, that he patented a diver's suit, or that his wife Bess would die while on a train ride. "This, too, shall pass away" was said to be the magician's lifelong mantra.

He departed the mortal coil after performing in spite of abdominal pain and a high fever from a ruptured *appendix* (from the Latin *appendere*, "to hang from something"). Unlike his Hermes self, his flesh could not traverse the worlds at will, and he died of peritonitis on Halloween, 1926. Oddly, he had just been touring with a bronze coffin, and he jokingly asked his wife to make use of it should the need arise. So she did.

Although his wife received no afterlife messages from him, the insurance company paid her a full double indemnity for his death. Hermes laughed again in 1953 when a film on Houdini's life starring Tony Curtis convinced generations of uncritical watchers that the great magician had died because of a failed Chinese Water Torture escape.

The archetypal trickster shows up in many, perhaps all, societies. Native Americans know him as Coyote, Hindus as Narada, ancient China as Lu Tung Pin, one of the Eight Immortals. He has been called Leprechaun, Dagonet, Gwyddion, Pa Pandir, Loki, Raven, Spider, and Al Khidr. Breaking up what is rigid, his passion for chaos leads to more flexible (and humorous) forms of understanding. Comedians and entertainers know him well; more to the point, they are known by him.

Mary Shelley

"Pandora" means "All-Gifted," and so she was. Fathered by Hephaestos, the blacksmith of the gods, she received wisdom from Athena, beauty from Aphrodite, and cleverness from Hermes. Grandfather Zeus had ordered her creation to punish hubristic Prometheus ("Foresight") for not giving proper obeisance to Olympus. As First Woman and intended bride to brother Epimetheus ("Hindsight"), she brought a jar (not a box) along with her. Prometheus warned his brother against opening the jar, but Pandora, who was curious, eventually did, loosing illness and death on the human race Prometheus had created. Although Zeus is often seen as vengeful here and Pandora as his wicked accomplice, what she really brought was mortality, and therefore the opportunity to feel vital and evolve. In this she is rightly compared to much-maligned Eve, whom the Gnostics regarded as the first Messenger of Light.

Mary Shelley's difficult birth deprived her of her mother. Her father, the liberal writer and philosopher William Godwin, provided her with little formal schooling but an unusually wide array of educational opportunities. By the time she was 19, when she set to work on her first and most famous novel, her multitalented mind had absorbed a great deal of classical literature, poetry, early feminism, science, history, philosophy, and politics.

While in Geneva during the terrifying storms of 1861, Mary and her paramour Percy Shelley worked opposite sides of the bringer of fire and animator of life. Percy saw Prometheus as a revolutionary figure and praised his courage in *Prometheus Unbound.* Mary Shelley had a nightmare about a monster brought to life (reanimation a recurring theme long abroad in alchemical Switzerland) and wrote *Frankenstein*, whose subtitle, *The Modern Prometheus*, referred not to the creature but to the creator.

The novel offers a critically Pandoran view of Promethean enthusiasm and its dreadful consequences. Pandora releases mortality and other limitations in accord with the will of heaven; the idealistic doctor recklessly opens the jar himself by attempting to take over the feminine prerogative of creation, with predictably disastrous results. His words might be required reading for every scientist tampering with the structure of matter and life:

> You seek for knowledge and wisdom, as I once did; and I ardently hope that the gratification of your wishes may not be a serpent to sting you, as mine has been....When I reflect that you are pursuing the same course, exposing yourself to the same dangers which have rendered me what I am, I imagine that you may deduce an apt moral from my tale...

Mary Shelley had plenty of encounters with mortality, for a long list of deaths surrounded her: her mother, Shelley's former wife, Percy himself, three of Mary's children, and a baby lost in a miscarriage. She never remarried, but the death of her father left her and young Percy, her only son, with improved financial prospects.

In myth a flood claimed humanity but spared Pyrrha, the daughter of Pandora. In Shelley's life her husband drowned in a squall and the worldwide disaster rose as a plague in her novel *The Last Man*.

When the jar of Pandora opened, an entity was left pulsing

inside: Hope, that which emerges as consolation for the last inundation and as warning about the next.

George Washington

Saturn has acquired a grim reputation, perhaps because he plays such a heavy in astrology. Associated with lead, melancholy, confinement, the color black, and the dreaded "Saturn Return," he remains the cold king who devoured his children. For the ancients, however, he also stood forth as a god of agriculture and plenty, and the harvest he oversaw led into a Golden Age of justice and fulfillment. His Roman temple contained the royal treasury. The Greeks called him Chronus (possibly from "to govern") and his wife Rhea, fellow cultivator of the harvest. The Norse knew him as beneficent Freyr, the Welsh as Amaethon, the Irish as Eochaid mac Eirc.

Black-garbed General Washington refused a literal crown, but he agreed to take up the presidency, coming down from Mount Vernon and parting with Martha with a certain understandable reluctance. Calm, commanding, and aloof, he was one of those fatherly men who keep being put in charge and who always do well once they are.

In the case of leading the Continental Army, Washington had combat experience and, although neither tactically nor strategically brilliant, had remained prudent in warfare, taking advantage of sudden opportunities and knowing how to use cover to hide from his British opponents, whom he served somewhat like sickle-wielding Chronus did after discovering himself to his tyrannical father Uranus.

In peacetime Washington retained the frugal intelligence of his mythic self and kept an eye on the local ecology. The story about cutting down the cherry tree is probably untrue but strikes an authentic agricultural note. A letter of Washington's from 1779 complains in Saturnian fashion that "We ruin the lands that are already cleared, and either cut down more wood, if we have it or emigrate into the western country...A half, a third or even a fourth of what land we mangle, well wrought and properly dressed, would produce more than the whole under our system of management...."

In most tellings Zeus overthrew Chronus, but in one variant the powerful Titan finally stepped aside in favor of his Olympian children. Ever orderly, the retired president rode his horse around his property every morning to inspect it.

That Washington owned slaves—lots of them—certainly fits the motif of the father eating his children. As though in protest, childless Washington's teeth all fell out in spite of constant brushing. Because of various legal complications and his unwillingness to further divide families, those slaves not yet freed remained in his service until after his death.

Washington died just three days before Saturnalia, the Roman celebration during which masters and slaves dined together in temporary peace, as though all men were created equal after all.

More Recent Mythic Lives

George W. Bush

"George" originally meant "farmer" in Greek, and indeed Ares (Mars) started out as an agricultural deity. A rancher of sorts. Horses were raced in his presence. He was also known as a protector of cattle.

Where George W. Bush and his advisers occupied the public stage they had seized, the Romans would have seen Mars with his ten-gallon helmet: Mars, the most reckless and impulsive of all old Jupiter's sons. Gods help us if he ever claimed his father's throne: Mars, who pursued battle for its own sake even when it clearly made no sense to. Terrible, tempestuous, inflexible Mars, whose companions were Phobos ("Fear"), Deimos ("Terror"), and their grim sister ~~Rice~~ Eris ("Strife"). Sometimes he had dark dealings with Pluto, the lethal and reclusive chief of Hades and keeper of treasures none were allowed to open.

James Hillman believes that some of us come in with a "bad seed," but how a myth manifests depends primarily on what we do with it. The Romans praised the courage and force of Mars to the extent of placing his image in the Roman Capitol. When appropriately channeled, the energy of Mars—or Ares to the ancient Greeks, Tyr to the Norse, Camulos to the Celts, Guan Yu to the Chinese—

fuels determination, assertiveness, and fierce protectiveness. You need Mars energy to stand up for yourself and your rights—unless you happen to be Cindy Sheehan or Athena, one of the few deities capable of knocking even Mars on his ass.

At first glance it might seem that America venerates Mars, but the truth is exactly the opposite. Most Americans have been taught to demonize martial emotions like anger so thoroughly that they have little choice but to build toward predictable eruptions. Political propaganda, the rhetoric of market fundamentalism, and the psychology industry have all convinced citizens enraged over the blatant oppression, hypocrisy, inequality, and injustice on daily display throughout our overmanaged nation that what they feel is *their* problem. As a result, a nation-sized pool of anger easily bursts into flagolatry and warfare once directed to external targets and projected outward. Life's battles are then fought out with literal bullets and bombs while the nation and its people collapse behind high borders.

At his best, Mars lights the fire within, sounds the alarm, wakes the soul from slumber and issues the order to march onward with life. At his worst he is Mars Ultor (Mars the Avenger), often followed by Enyo, "Horror," destroyer of cities. Trust unreflective Mars, or Bush Decider, to fight fire with and for gasoline in order to promote the general warfare. Mars never negotiates and cannot be reasoned with. He acts without thinking and often without feeling. He would not understand why "surge" would be the operative word in "insurgency." Instead, he thanks the centurions "who wear the uniform for your sacrifice" while his compromised colleagues look on in shameful silence.

John Denver

The boyish-looking man born Henry John Deutschendorf was no stranger to vehicular mishaps. In 1993 he was arrested for driving under the influence, and a year later he drove his Porsche into a tree. In 1989 he survived a plane crash. This son of an Air Force test pilot was even born near a crash, if an officially discounted one: Roswell, New Mexico, where to this day witnesses claim a UFO went down.

At the time of his death in a plane crash over Monterey Bay, Denver had been grounded for the DUIs. He was neither drunk when he went up nor flying legally, his license and medical certificate having been suspended. As with the other incidents, as with Aspen, where he sometimes cut the engine for a glide to fill up his senses, he must have believed, as do all striving for exteriorized immortality, that he of all people would not be caught. It makes a kind of mythic sense that his second wife's name was Cassandra, issuer of unregarded warnings.

Some men sense the end before it comes, most often those seeming to harbor some deep-down demon who pushes to bring it about. A week before the crash, Denver, who had promised friends and family he would take fewer risks during his flights, had left an amusing message on his brother's voicemail: "This is God calling. Just wanted to...just wanted to [laughter] see how you were doing." The name of an album he was working on at the time: *All Aboard*. It followed songs with titles like "Looking for Space" and "The Wings That Fly Us Home." And of course his first hit long ago had been "Leavin' on a Jet Plane."

When father Daedalus fashioned fragile wings of reeds, feathers, and wax, he warned his pilot son about their limitations; but like so many boundless optimists, Icarus, who had no patience for limitations, flew higher and higher until the sun melted the wax. So the wings fell apart, their center could not hold, and the brash boy arrowed into the sea. According to federal investigators, Denver took off with too little fuel in his forward tank. A stuck valve prevented him from switching to his backup tank. In such a manner did an ancient piece of mythology work itself out to its saddest conclusion over the depths of Monterey Bay in 1997.

Phoolan Devi

Once upon a time a girl who grew up poor in India decided not to be a victim anymore of sexual assaults perpetrated by upper-class males, including (some say) her husband. She began to fight back.

She fought back so successfully that local bandits began to seek her out. When they captured her, their brutal leader made the fatal mistake of trying to rape her. She killed him and took over the gang.

As she learned from them and began to lead them, leaving a bloody trail of would-be attackers in her wake, a legend began to circulate that she was a reincarnation of the goddess Durga, a form of the great all-goddess Devi. The Bandit Queen made sure to thank Durga's image after every successful upper-caste kidnap and raid.

In every pantheon lurk troublesome beings, whether Frost Giants, trolls, water horses, or Yeti. In ancient Hindu lore the demons were getting out of hand, so the gods got together to create a goddess capable of handling them. Ancient depictions of Durga wielding a sword shouldn't look like modern murals of Phoolan Devi holding a rifle, but they do. From Durga's fierce brow emanated black Kali.

Eventually the police caught up with Phoolan Devi, and after a long trial she went to prison. While incarcerated she underwent a hysterectomy. (Athena, Durga's Greek counterpart, was a virgin.) When she got out, such was the force of her influence that she claimed a seat in Parliament.

In 2001 she was assassinated outside her New Delhi residence by men who claimed the right to avenge some of the deaths she had caused. Had she lived her myth too literally and been possessed by it? Had she betrayed it by becoming a politician? Something of both? Hard to say; but it's likely that the last sound she heard was one of the bullets that struck her fiercely lined forehead.

Jodie Foster

Although actors get typecast into certain recurring roles, when a myth is involved the roles tend not to stay in the script.

A target of numerous stalkers both on and off screen, Foster was raised by her mother much as Persephone was raised by Demeter. (Foster's wealthy father had vanished.) Innocent as a lamb, Persephone found herself jerked down into the underworld one day and molested by dark Pluto, the god of secret treasure, who had a fondness for hiding beneath his cap of invisibility. As a result, she spent part of the year married to him and part of it bringing spring back into a grateful, blossoming world.

This plotline of being captured and transformed by the captor recurs in Foster's films. Pluto figures on screen include the terrorist in *Flightplan*, Hannibal Lector, an entire gang of rapists in *The Accused*, the armed robbers in *Panic Room*, the killer she hunts in *The Brave One*, *Contact*'s David Drumlin, who descends into the underworld himself, and Michael Kitz from the same film, played by an actor who provided the voice for Pluto in a Disney film.

"Why me?" Foster asked in an article written after being stalked by John Hinckley. It's a good question. Persephone had probably asked it too. The answer, in general, seems to be: To gain Pluto's capacity for night vision. To gain underworld insight. The Zeus-like S. R. Hadden in *Contact* might have been speaking to everyone crossed by myth when he said, "There it was all the time, staring you in the face..."

Foster, who said that as a child actress she had to fight for her life or get gobbled up, has also spoken in interviews about her understandably ambivalent feelings about men. Even now the father of her children remains invisible.

James ("He Who Supplants") Hillman

How an archetypal figure manifests, whether positively or negatively, depends on the quality of our relationship with it. From an inquiring consciousness even the devil deserves his luciferian "Light Bringer" due.

If the devil (a mythological composite with a strong Hades component) were to get himself reborn in the U.S., an Atlantic City hotel room might just do the trick. Penetrating and witty, he would probably include in his education a stint in the armed services for a close-up look at the deviltry of warfare. Pathology, amorality, and decay would fascinate him, and so they should, for he would view them through the perspective of the underworld, where everything gets reversed. Down there sickness, mortification, rot, but not health, set the primary if grim standard of psychic value.

Hillman loves to reverse things, from the tree image of development standing on its head with roots in the sky to life itself as a downward journey and never an upward climb. One of his tools of reversal and inversion is rhetoric, always a strong point of the horned gent from below. Not only does he take archetypal image for archetype, the move Jung wearily inveighed against, he has made this move a cornerstone of what is now called "archetypal psychology" even though it really represents a return less to archetype than to myth, in actual practice a mythopoetic psychology that tends the nonhuman through considerations deeply humane. There's an audacity in that. Hillman's writing never lacks his engaging adeptness for turning things inside out and upside down, and he always speaks with refreshing brilliance and charm. Who'd have guessed that paganism needed an evangelist?

Of course, going to Hades is far easier than getting out. One even gets used to being down there. Archetypalists favor no ascents, no heroic journeys into the light. They seldom tire of talking and writing about disaster, gloom, rupture, anguish, and catastrophe, latent or manifest. Even dream symbols must remain in the underworld, where they remain free to enjoy a near-total separation from the dayworld. But Hillman writes and speaks about "soul"? Well, of course he does! The devil is fascinated by soul. Sell him yours and you can stay downstairs forever, agreeing with Hillman that hope is indeed an evil. "Abandon All Hope, Ye Who Enter Here" could be one of the mottos of archetypal psychology. No to hope, alas, but yes to beauty, Aphrodite having been appreciated by old Hades himself.

Bad seed. War's inevitability. Depression as prescription. Fragmentation's ubiquity. To these recurring devilish themes Hillman adds that "images don't stand for anything." Naturally not. Part of the underworld's power comes from its eternal dreamy mix of image with imaged, for as in Los Angeles, the copy is held as more real than the copied. The devil would not impress anyone if he failed to confuse the two. The very term for this is delightfully inverted: "psychic reality."

As Pacifica Graduate Institute, a gathering place for archetypal psychology, opened its new Santa Barbara campus, it took over what used to be a rather roomy church sitting over an underworld of ancient catacombs. High on walls bearing panels of stained glass were hung a trinity of large posters bearing the likenesses of Jung,

Marija Gimbutas, and Hillman.

I wonder at times whether it amuses him, seeing his face up high in a chapel once devoted to worship of the Redeemer.

Timothy Levitch

In 1998, New Yorker Timothy "Speed" Levitch, a bus tour guide for Gray Line Tours, starred in the documentary *The Cruise*. Displaying a profound knowledge of the city through his amusing rapid-fire patter, Levitch walked, gesticulated, and rode his talk of delighting in the world's (and his own) aliveness. In one scene he compares the sensuality of terracotta to running naked after the woman of his desire; in another he hugs the Brooklyn Bridge like a friend; in yet another, he talks about the intense presence of the city, its infrastructure angry with him for whatever reason ("I thought we were getting a divorce") but evidently placated by a revamping and revitalizing of his tour through the skyscraper-enshadowed soul of Manhattan.

Levitch, who stays nowhere permanently, sleeps on friends' sofas and writes poetry. He uses "Cruising" as a conscious metaphor of the motion that keeps the spirit alive and out of the grips of the "Anti-Cruise," the cultural inertia that lays like a gray city grid plan over the enthusiasm and joyfulness that humans inherit as a birthright but too often forfeit.

Dancing his way across Manhattan, Levitch stands at last beneath the Twin Towers (the film was made before 9/11/2001). Staring upward, he suggests spinning around in circles, then suddenly lying down on the ground. Doing this makes the buildings look like they are falling. Lord Shiva might have agreed.

Toward the end of the film, Levitch, who is Jewish, describes the Lamed Vovniks, the Thirty-Six hidden people whose presence here keeps God from destroying the world and starting over. Vovniks tend to be poor or retarded, and most do not know who they are, yet the role their suffering plays in holding things together earns them the appellation of Men of Perfect Equilibrium.

According to an old story (as told by Levitch), a certain outhouse cleaner named Mordecai visited the Baal Shem Tov, the rabbi who founded Hasidism and helped infuse it with joy and celebration. Yet Mordecai danced with such abandon that the embarrassed gatherers kicked him out. So he sought out the lepers instead and danced for them at midnight. The following morning, when a rumor spread that a Vovnik was in the area, Mordecai had vanished. Followers and students found only the Baal Shem Tov, who wept because of the man now known as the Dancer of God: "He was healthy among the sick, and I did not see him."

Was Levitch telling his own myth? Gray Line management might have liked to know, but when they went to find him, he had disappeared.

Marilyn Monroe

Marilyn Monroe, originally named Norma after a star-crossed lover, has been compared so often with Aphrodite and Venus that an explanation might seem superfluous. Yes, she was lovely, and yes, charismatic and curvy, but the smile opening in her eyes and lighting up her face was what most immediately conveyed the aphroditic blessing, especially to those who witnessed it in person.

Because of how the Romans took over the Greek pantheon, appropriating it rather than reflecting on it in any depth, the shadow versions of the Greek gods often appear most clearly in their Roman counterparts. (Mars might be an exception: honored and valorized in Rome, he seems to cut a bolder and nobler path than careless, destructive Ares.) In Roman Empire culture the lightness, sunshine, and sheer fun of Aphrodite degenerated into the worldly, acquisitive seductiveness of Venus.

This shift seems to have spread itself across Monroe's life as well, with success and exploitation pressuring her into sexual power plays, questionable business arrangements, and petulant acts of vanity. Ultimately, her natural Aphroditic-Venusian attraction to martial strife set her up for affairs with dangerous men, one of whom might well have murdered her. The details of her death remain unresolved, and the private journal she was known to have kept was never found.

Unable to see through the bars of her myth, she lived Venus's many affairs concretely instead of refashioning the connections they symbolized into more thoughtful acts of bridge-building and outreach: deeper strengths of Aphrodite's power of attraction. Men in locker rooms ogled her as her real talents—and she had many—went almost unnoticed. But then it has never been easy to shine forth the archetypal power of love in murky Hollywood, a violent subculture whose real deity in chief has always been Narcissus.

Diana Mountbatten-Windsor, Princess of Wales

Imagine what it must be like for someone born into the myth of attention-avoiding Diana the Hunter (the Greek Artemis) to marry a prince and find herself in the spotlight.

A daughter of royalty, Princess Diana and her brother learned early on to look out for each other, as had Artemis and Apollo. But Artemis/Diana spent most of her time in the company of young women when she wasn't out riding and looking after the animals of her forest. The princess went to a girls' school in Kent, and although her grades were never outstanding, she took an ardent interest in athletics, including swimming and riding horses.

The marriage to Prince Charles made political sense, but it went against the grain of the myth. Diana the "virgin" goddess did have lovers, but as a personification of the undomesticatable spirit of nature, she conducted her relationships entirely at her discretion. Diana the Princess also had lovers, but her world remained tragically unprotected from powerful masculine influences. To escape them she sometimes disguised herself and walked the streets of London at night. It's hardly surprising that one of her affairs would include her riding instructor.

Her marital separation and divorce opened up some sanctuary space while allowing her to remain a member of the royal family. Just as the maternal goddess looked after newborns, being a patroness of childbirth, the princess took up the cause of eliminating landmines in order to safeguard the world's children. She admired strong women and saw a feminist therapist. Her acquaintances were considered unconventional by the standards of British high society. She continued to spend time with them anyway.

Mythic incidents almost never relive themselves the same way twice. In antiquity the hunter Acteon stumbled upon a sacred grove of Diana. She was bathing nude in a pool with some of her nymphs. Noticing him, she splashed him with water, causing him to turn into a stag. He fled but was tracked down and torn apart by his own hungry hounds.

In August of 1997, Princess Diana and her lover, wealthy film producer Dodi Al-Fayed, died in a car accident in a tunnel: archetypally, a narrow, dim place of transition. They had previously picked out an engagement ring together and had recently spent time on his yacht. And although we will never know whether the princess could have remained true to herself and her myth while pursuing this romance through realms of wealth and power, this time the hounds came for them both as baying paparazzi giving motorized mad pursuit.

Oprah Winfrey

> Now I wish you to know about the strangest thing ever found anywhere in written texts or in human memory.... I tell you that on the right-hand side of the Indies there was an island called California, which was very close to the region of the Terrestrial Paradise. This island was inhabited by black women, and there were no males among them at all, for their life style was similar to that of the Amazons. The island was made up of the wildest cliffs and the sharpest precipices found anywhere in the world. These women had energetic bodies and courageous, ardent hearts, and they were very strong.

Some myths seem to require their bearer to be in the right place.

One of the inspirations for the colonization of California was a popular knights-in-armor novel published in 1510. In *The Exploits of Esplandian* (*Las Sergas de Esplandian*) by Garcia Rodriguez Ordoñez de

Montalvo, a heroic knight named Esplandian teamed up with his father Amadis to face off against the warrior women of an island called California. Among its gold-armored inhabitants buzzed fabulous griffins, condorlike Arabian birds who dropped conquistadors from high up and then ate them. They also ate the Amazons' male children shortly after they were born. Strangely enough, the place that would be named California after mighty Queen Calafia's fabulous island was represented on maps as an island even after explorers and cartographers had proved it was not.

Oprah Winfrey, a queen of sorts in her own right, was born in Mississippi and raised in Milwaukee, but she eventually made her way to California, touted for centuries as a paradise on earth, and took over a Montecito spread called The Promised Land. She also owns homes on two actual islands and thinks of the students at the Oprah Winfrey Leadership Academy for Girls as her daughters. No dangerous griffins fly over Oprah in Santa Barbara, but a benign Angel Network reaches out internationally to support and fund charitable projects.

Queen Calafia, the most prominent and powerful of all the Amazons of California Isle, eventually ended up with the brave knight Esplandian for a mate. As versions of the knight passed through Oprah's early life, at least two of them predicted that she would launch a promising public career.

Mythic Miscellany

Below are odds, ends, and wonderings to go with the guesswork above.

One of the people who has written about personal myth is philosopher Sam Keen. In his book on the topic he never specifies a particular myth for himself, but he does mention a childhood fascination with a monkey his father carved for him. What is that monkey's story? He shows up in Keen's playful style, in his eagerness to swing from idea to idea, and in the fact that Keen loves to bounce on the trapeze.

Pacifica graduate Sophia Heller has written *The Absence of Myth* to argue that we moderns can live just fine without mythological shenanigans; but, having plunged down from heaven into the sublunar hell of materialism, isn't this exactly what the Gnostic figure of fallen Sophia would maintain?

Is Al Gore standing in the shadow of Merlin? His solutions to the environmental crisis tend to be technological. When he appeared holographically at the Live Earth concert in 2007, the pun word "algorithm" kept running through my mind. Of course he doesn't want to be in charge. That's Arthur's job.

Does Zeus permeate Sean Connery's life or just show up for his film roles as King Arthur, Agamemnon, Richard Lionheart, and various male authorities? Does Hermes follow Tom Hanks through crash landings, airports, and aborted space missions? Did he follow Orson Welles, who pulled off the famous "War of the Worlds" radio skit for Mercury Theatre? What is going on with Arnold Schwarzenegger, who not only starred as a machine but treats his own body like one?

What about Clint Eastwood and his "man with no name": in other words Hades, who painted a town red and, entering *Pale Rider*, took off his hat and became invisible to his enemies? Carmel seems a natural place for Hades to become mayor: ensconced in Monterey, it began as an artist colony until several of the artists killed themselves. An early shipment of home-building supplies delivered only doors. To where? Ocean Avenue used to be nicknamed the Devil's Staircase.

Speaking of film, Maeve Quinlan's erotic scene with young James Bullard in the controversial 2002 movie *Ken Park* brings to mind Queen Maeve's attempt to seduce young Cuchulainn in an incident out of Irish folklore. The name of Bullard's character was Shawn, another Irish name. A bit of the myth unconsciously reenacted?

Dr. Martin Luther King Jr.: not the first or the last king to fall in Memphis, a city named after the ancient capital of Egypt. Another courageous leader of that time, Malcolm X, rose to prominence on the ashes of a murdered father and a destroyed childhood. He renamed himself El Hajj Malik El-Shabazz after his pilgrimage to Mecca, but the name "Malcolm" derives from a prince of Scotland who took the throne after King Lear murdered his father. Ossie Davis beautifully eulogized him in Harlem as "our own shining black prince."

IT MIGHT SEEM FROM THESE SNAPSHOTS that a life can be explained by its personal myth, but framing a similar argument for one's ancestry, DNA, or basic temperament shows its lack of weight. Nor does a personal myth involve a single protagonist who operates alone. Tracing a myth invariably involves unearthing an entire constellation of interacting characters, each of whom requires research to substantiate, as does the myth as a whole. Liking computers or hammers doesn't make someone a Hephaestos, nor would any DSM-style checklist help (e.g., five parallels between your life and the myth confirm the myth, but four do not). Feeling the fit of a myth requires a certain imaginative intuition, and doing the necessary research grounds the intuition in solid exploration.

A myth is what we make of it, nothing more and nothing less; and what we can make of it blossoms into new possibilities for living when we learn what mythic story we are in.

CHAPTER 3

Uncovering Your Myth

We have only to glance around to see how broken mythologies make for broken people and places: Paranoid voyeurs spying on citizens under the tired old mythos of National Security. Industrialists peering out at destroyed landscapes through the digitized mask of the dysfunctional totem Progress. Nuclear-armed Puritans touting the myth of the Nuclear Family while wrecking the economic foundations of real families. The delusional, as Bill Moyers put it so well, is no longer marginal in our day. Neither is plutocracy—as in Pluto, deadly god of underworldly wealth, last seen turning the surface of an ailing planet into a literal underworld.

Meanwhile the psychology industry continues to crank out fad therapies sold with the same capitalistic exuberance as new diets. The diets promise quick loss of weight, the fads quick replacement of "negative" emotions by "self-esteem." New and improved, revolutionary breakthrough; discern the opportunity in the crisis, buzzes the rusty saw—but not the crisis of opportunism.

With the meaning systems of religion, politics, economics, and therapeutics descending into nihilistic bankruptcy, we find ourselves invited to reexamine and remember the ancient stories that have always guided humanity in times of darkness. The ancient Greeks, for example, told of the Argus, a hundred-eyed monster that served as a perfect mass surveillance device. Even the muscular and heroic gods were afraid of the power of its unceasing vigilance. But Hermes the Trickster had a different approach. Instead of taking the thing on in battle, he sat down in plain sight of it and began to play on a lyre. So soothingly did he play that all the eyes gradually closed. With the monster lulled to sleep by inaction, Hermes moved in and cut off its head.

The old stories can also give us a context for tracking down our personal myth by helping us turn life events into plot motifs.

In the comedy film *Stranger than Fiction* (dir. Marc Forster, 2006), an IRS agent named Harold Crick consults a professor of literature because a female voice no one else can hear has begun to narrate Harold's daily life. (He had consulted a therapist first, but she told him he was schizophrenic and needed to go on medication.) After Professor Hilbert asks a number of strange questions ("Have you ever been the king of anything? Is it possible that at one time you were made of wood, stone, lye, buried corpse parts, or earth made holy by rabbinical elders?"), he explains to his bewildered visitor that in order to find out his story, he needs to learn which stories Harold is *not* in. "Odd as it may seem, I've just ruled out half of Greek literature, seven fairy tales, ten Chinese fables, and determined conclusively that you are not King Hamlet, Scout Finch, Miss Marple, Frankenstein's monster, or a golem. Aren't you relieved to know you're not a golem?"

Although the Hilbert method does not succeed, it can furnish those of us who lack the convenience of an audible narrator a humorous reminder of the need to know a wide range of stories in order to find out more about our own. Instead of going through all of world lore and literature, however, we can encourage the right story to show up and corroborate the one we now live.

Suggestions for Tracking Your Myth

Following are some methods and ideas that have worked for seekers on the trail of their myth. They are geared to make visible what story one is living. They do not constitute a lesson book or program because how a myth reveals itself tends not to conform to any curriculum but its own.

1. Read Stories, Watch Movies, Absorb Many Myths...

....and as you expose yourself to as many stories as you can (pick the ones that find you: it's amazing how they can just fall into your hands), check in with your feelings and your body to find out which stories, characters, and plot twists resonate strongly with you. Pay most attention to the story elements that bring up a lot of emotion and recognition: *This is me. This is my story.* Imagine yourself into the action. Is some of it happening to you right now in symbolic form?

It's very important to stay with what carries energy for you because otherwise the sheer number and variety of stories in the world can feel quite overwhelming. Collect the ones that interest you, bother you, make you curious to know more and leave the rest aside for now.

If you find yourself sorting through stories of gods and goddesses, be critical of two common classifications often imposed by anthropologists in too big a hurry: "warrior deity" and "fertility deity." Odin and Morrigan are often mislabeled war or battle deities, for example, and almost every goddess under the sun or moon has been called a fertility deity at one time or another. For a clearer sense of a deity's style, acquire your own familiarity.

2. Take a Deeper Look Into Your Names and How You Got Them.

What's in a name? At the very least a story or two. For example, it's odd how often people with a vocation related to nature have some nature right in their names. My first name, Craig, means "an outcropping of stone," and my last name is Americanized Swedish: the "quist" part means "small branch." My birth father's last name has the word "land" in it; my birth mother's middle name is a place name in England. Look up what your names mean. If you have a Christianized name this can be a bit trickier because most baby name books will go back to the Christian meaning and stop there. Look deeper into the origins of your name and see if what you learn resonates.

Whether your name bears an obvious connection to your myth depends in part on the logic of the myth. In some cases work is required to trace the connection. In other cases, like Rebecca's (see

Chapter 4), the myth is obvious in the name. Still others will find it in the name they were almost given. Some have rejected their first name and gone by their middle name, only to learn that the first name evoked a personal myth they were not ready to face earlier. When younger I disliked my middle name for the same reason. Ask parents and family members for the story of your name: the circumstances surrounding it, how it occurred to them, what their fantasies were about the name, what they almost named you and why.

3. Find Out Your Birth Story and Reimagine It as a Creation Story.

People who hear about my birth story often tell me it's unique. I have found, however, that everyone's birth story contains some quirk, some hidden fact or unusual plot line. You might have to dig a bit to find it, but it's there and it could unlock your myth. It might be something simple, like a woman named Diana, goddess of childbirth, learning that she helped her mother give birth to her brother. Or a funny anecdote, or something the delivering doctor said, or a fantasy that occurred to your mother during the delivery. Everyone comes in marked or heralded.

To deepen this exploration, try writing down two versions of your birth story. The first should be "objective" and factual: "I was born at 8:54 p.m. in Walnut Creek, California, during a record-breaking drought...." etc. This is the style we've grown used to through our imagination-destroying educational system. Now rewrite it like a fable or screenplay in a "once upon a time" style that evokes the drama and feeling of the event. Lay out the plot and the characters, and show how the miracle—and every birth is a miracle—impacted everyone as someone entirely unique entered the world.

Incidentally, if you were born into shabby circumstances, you're in good company: so was many a Redeemer and Hero figure. Orphanage is another frequent motif, as the birth stories of Moses and King Arthur remind us.

4. Examine Your First Memories and Dreams.

As Alfred Adler noted long ago, first memories often carry basic themes that play out over an entire lifetime. We remember what fits and supports our script. A lifelong theme of breaking out of confinement showed up in many of my early dreams, in an early memory of grabbing the bars of a crib in mute protest at being confined there, and even in having grown up in El Cajon, literally "The Box," a conservative San Diegan city whose tallest building was the jail.

5. Track Your Early Obsessions.

Very often we are drawn to see and hear the same bedtime stories, fairy tales, books, TV shows, or films over and over throughout childhood because they contain aspects of our myth. Find out which stories you kept bugging an adult to read or retell, make a list of shows or films or books you couldn't get enough of, and look for common plot elements and recurring motifs among them. Which characters could you relate to? Which did you fear or want to avoid? Most importantly, how and where do they show up in your life today?

Look also for odd situations you'd never have consciously decided to be involved in. In elementary school I was chosen to be on local TV to give a brief explanation of how the Indians of California had used tules to make watertight seacraft. At that time I felt no interest in the topic and much perplexity about how I'd been talked into speaking about it publicly. I would never have guessed that as an adult I would write a large book on the history of "Deep California," some of it devoted to how the state's original inhabitants had resisted colonization and preserved precious aspects of their culture intact.

6. Note the Objects, Images, and Animals You Collected.

I have a lifelong fascination with alchemy, the search for the fabulous red Philosopher's Stone capable of bestowing health and turning base metals into gold. Jung believed alchemy and its symbols to be a forerunner of his version of depth psychology. Alchemy also plays an important part in *terrapsychology*, the study of our deep connections to the places where we live and to the things and creatures inhabiting them.

All I knew as a child, however, was that red stones, plumbing, and the insides of machines fascinated me, as did stylized representations of the sun, moon, and stars. Scientifically accurate depictions of celestial objects also interested me, but my real passion was for animated images of them: Sun and Moon with faces or crowns, stars as lively glowing bodies. When I failed to persuade my parents to buy me a stellar mobile like the one I saw at a friend's, I made my own. Its smiling Sun and Moon spun for years above my bed without my knowing them to symbolize Sol and Luna, the King and Queen of alchemy.

The Phoenix has also followed me around. In alchemy it symbolizes the end of the work, with the Dragon standing at its beginning. In childhood I did not know what a phoenix was, but I drew pictures of flaming purple birds and was caught taking peacock feathers from a neighbor's yard. Normally so unwilling to arouse the ire of adults, I just had to have some of those colorful feathers. The mythic self refused to take "no" for an answer.

7. Look for the Mythic Background to Important Life Events.

To an eye sensitive to symbol and image, milestones and turning points reveal storied dimensions normally invisible to thinking that clings to the literal surface of things. When I was training to be a therapist, we were in group supervision when one of the trainees mentioned that his last client had forgotten her pink shades. We all had an appreciative laugh over her unconscious signal of leaving behind the need to see the world through rose-colored glasses.

Wide reading combined with sensitivity to the symbolism in key events in your life will enable you to recognize their mythic elements. Common mythic elements include:

A second (divine) set of parents
A birth preceded by a death
Receiving a second or secret name
Close calls with death
Abduction or kidnapping
The call to adventure

The fall from paradise
Underworld journey
Heroic quest
The helping animal(s)
Shapeshifting
Retrieval of a Prize or magical object
Helping or being helped by a magical being
Taking a leadership role early on
Discovering a new realm
Killing a mortal enemy
Living a secret double life
Trickster encounters
The nonhuman lover
The intergenerational curse
Exile and homecoming
Imprisonment/Limbo
Breakout
Betrayal
The great meeting
The search
Taking the medicine
Threshold or passageway
The contest or climax
The apocalypse
The turning point or reversal
The resolution
Apotheosis (becoming godlike)

When you come across one of these situations, take it into the world of fantasy and let it play out in a daydream. Go with it watchfully for a while, step in when you have a solid visualization building itself in your consciousness, and follow along wherever the characters or action decide to lead you. Making art from within this type of reverie can bring these situations vividly to life.

8. *Look for Typical Mythical Characters in Your Life's Drama.*
For example:

Vampires (can't help them)
Sleeping beauties
Hidden queens and kings
Helpers
Hinderers (speedbumps on the heroic journey)
Saints
Heroes and antiheroes
Outcasts
Orphans
Wanderers
Curmudgeons
Cheer-bringers
Flatterers
Spies
Seers/Prophets/Fortune tellers
World-weary investigators
Tricksters
Court jesters
Performers
Artists
Strong Men/Women
Seducers
Converts
Wizards/Magicians
Witches/Priestesses
Rebels
Heretics
Martyrs
Wise Old Man/Crone
Divine Children
The Other Lover
The Betrayer (Iago-Judas types)
Warriors (male or female)
Emissaries/Ambassadors/Peacemakers

The Crowd (does whatever loudmouths tell them)
Chieftains/Warlords
Apprentices
The Greek Chorus (commenting from off stage)
Substitute Parents
Evil Step-Siblings
Otherworldly beings: ghosts, spirit guides, fairies, etc.
Animal guides

9. Search Your Relationships.

Look for stories you play over and over in your relationships. What part do you keep playing? Who, mythically speaking, is your partner again and again? Are you Persephone repeatedly getting pulled down into the underworld by one dark Hades after another? Inanna being hung up on a hook? Artemis killing her lover Orion "by accident?" Samson having his hair cut off?

Bear in mind that in any two-person relationship, romantic or otherwise, at least two stories are involved. The woman who is Penelope to my Odysseus might be Demeter mourning her lost daughter in terms of her own tale. The roles interlock, however. Demeter and Penelope share things in common. If I play Ares to an Aphrodite but King Arthur to myself, I can see some of myself in the role I play in my partner's story by remembering that Arthur could be warlike, that Camelot was named after Camulos, the Celtic war god, and there's always been more than a touch of Aphrodite in Guinevere.

10. Ask Your Dreams.

"Dream incubation" means going to bed at night, getting comfortable, and asking the other side (the unconscious, the mythic realm, the what-have-you: pick a descriptor) for a dream about your myth. What turns up will depend among other things on whether you are in a good place to receive the information. Some dreamers have been told straight out what their myth is. One woman dreamed that someone called out to her, "Diana!" Her researches confirmed this as her myth.

Sometimes it's that direct, but other times you receive just enough—an image, a plot line—to go back to the stories with to seek for more parallels and resonances. The myth does want to be known, but it may require work, especially if it would present you with a heavy burden at a difficult time.

11. Examine Your Natal Chart.

There are different ways to hold astrology. One need not believe that the planets exert a significant and literal causal effect on human doings. Jung's hypothesis of synchronicity provides an alternative: that because everything is connected to everything else, then the moment I was born, the configurations in the heavens at that time, and the applicable systems of symbolism worked out over many centuries all share common elements that can be interpreted meaningfully.

Again, go by what resonates. If it makes sense to you that a lot of natal action in your Twelfth House of trouble, secrets, and old business indicates a strong underworld motif in your life, then explore that possibility. If you find yourself repeatedly rescuing people, have a look at where the wounded healer Chiron is in your chart, and at who allies with him and who frustrates him. Where is your Sun (identity) and Moon (emotions) and North Node (direction)? These can provide hints and clues if you treat them as puzzle pieces to mix in with the growing accumulation of clues.

12. What Are Your Responses to the Big Questions?

How you answer the big questions of life can say a lot about your myth. Why? Because we often answer from within our mythic story, from the temple or altar of a particular storied perspective. Ask Mars what he thinks of love and he's liable to say it's a battlefield, whereas Isis would probably emphasize devotion and a knack for never giving up on a loved one. Coyote would shake it and see what falls out. Ask yourself some of the big questions—What would I give my life for? Why am I here? What do I have faith in? What do I love? What can't I tolerate? Who is my clan, who are my kindred?"—and sift your responses through the filter of another key question: What kind of character, god, mythic figure would respond this way?

13. If At First You Don't Succeed, Try Another Pantheon.

Myths and archetypes appear in many forms and faces. If you have some sense of your myth but aren't quite satisfied with the version you're familiar with, look for similar versions elsewhere. For example, if you resonate with some aspects of Hera but not others, have a look at her Irish parallel Morrigan, a being on equal terms with her Allfather husband the Dagda, or at all-seeing Frigg, consort to Odin. If Dionysus fits in some ways but lacks the exact feeling of the death-rebirth motif in your life, study and feel into Osiris, brought back to life by a goddess rather than a god. If Baubo, the lecherous dancer who amused Demeter, doesn't quite fit, look into outgoing Ame-no-Uzume, who started the commotion that helped draw the insulted sun goddess Amaterasu out of her cave.

The deep psyche makes use of the story that will get through to you regardless of where it comes from. If your sense is that you have not quite found it, then you are probably correct. Keep looking, reading, feeling, dreaming. You're already in the myth: it's just a matter of recognizing which one, as the following personal accounts will demonstrate.

CHAPTER 4

Accounts of Personal Myth Work

The following firsthand accounts were written by former students and seminar participants invited to tell some of their tale for this book.

Inanna's Descent

The Sumerian goddess Inanna decides to leave her comfortable post in heaven and earth one day to journey to the underground. Before she leaves, she instructs her most trusted female assistant to seek help from the gods to secure her return if she does not come back in three days. With that, she prepares herself with special clothing and accessories and descends to the land of no return.

At the gate she is met by her sister Ereshkigal's gatekeeper and asks for entrance. He consults Ereshkigal, who responds with anger at this intrusion and instructs the gatekeeper to admit her but to treat her like anyone else who comes to her dark realm.

Inanna is led through seven gates, and at each gate a piece of her beautiful clothing or an exquisite accessory is taken from her so that at the last gate she arrives naked and bowed low.

She is then brought to Ereshkigal. In an act that infuriates her sister, Inanna sits on her throne.

For this she is judged by seven judges and beaten to death, and her corpse is hung on a peg to rot. Three days go by, so her trusted assistant Ninshubur follows Inanna's instructions and visits the gods to beg for help in releasing Inanna. Finally one agrees. From the dirt under his fingernails he creates two mourners to slip into the underworld and befriend Ereshkigal. They find her in pain from mourning or birth and earn her trust and gratitude by keeping her company during her ordeal. When she asks them what they would like as a gift of thanks, they say they want the rotting flesh of Inanna. They remove her from the peg and restore her to life before ascending from the underworld.

In a grand play orchestrated by archetypal patterns, I have met my Ereshkigal and have identified myself with Inanna's energy and myth.

A concrete example of the impact of this myth in my life is my own descent, my own face-to-face time with Ereshkigal and the final ascent from her underworld. It was life-altering, and my time in the underworld enduring the harsh demands of Ereshkigal lasted for many long, painful months. I, like, Inanna, enjoyed the success in the upperworld of fruitful creativity and power. However, balance will be demanded in the universe, so Ereshkigal reached up from her dark world of the unknown and dragged me down, rattled me to my core and unceremoniously tossed me onto the hook.

I know a woman in my life who personifies Ereshkigal and brings the ongoing cosmic themes of this myth into play in my life in various ways. When we met, both of us were strong and successful career women just starting our families and enrolled in Lamaze classes. We both gave birth to baby girls with the same first name and delivered within hours of each other in delivery rooms next to each other in the hospital. She was "on her throne" as president of a bank, and prior to meeting me had not encountered another woman she considered a peer. She was very identified with her career position and judged everything against this standard. I was also "on my throne" in my career as founder and technical officer of my company but was not as identified with the position. For me it was more play (like Inanna), and for her it was more burden (like Ereshkigal). I was light, creation and energy as an inventor and she was analysis, fact and "reality" as a banker. Many powerful things occurred between the two of us, and only now, with the descent of Inanna fresh in my psyche, can I put some of them into a broader perspective for the first time.

I hired her to work for my company. As I invented products, markets and opportunities. I was not aware that brewing within her was the desire to do the same, to be recognized as a creative force as well and to have more influence on my "upperworld" realm. She must have filled with envy, rage, and self-pity, because these are the same dark emotions she caused to well up in me, intense, unknown and wholly unrecognized. It was as if she said bitterly "Welcome to my world..." as the depth of those dark emotions rudely invaded my interior space. At the time I could not understand her underhanded, passive-aggressive behavior. Today, with my new sight, I can see her anguish and can imagine for the first time the depth of her own suffering in relation to what I brought forth for her. I clearly see now the mythological pattern that was playing out.

Things came to a head through various business and financial turns of fate.

In the end through my descent I was forced to see, assimilate and own the dark emotions emanating from her Ereshkigal energies, which pushed me into claiming the repressed parts of my femininity that had gone underground, unconscious. There was of course reciprocity involved. She learned to embrace the Inanna energies I held for her and ended up founding two companies of her own. She also balanced and reclaimed her feminine fertility, bringing intuitive creativity into her career. Interestingly, the two companies she started remain dependent on the technology I invented. It is as if a piece of me, a surrogate for me, is still there with her. This too mirrors the myth, for at the end of Inanna's descent, Ereshkigal agrees to let Inanna ascend if she brings back a surrogate to take her place in the Great Below. Inanna complies.

The result of my descent for me was actually a beginning: a new life, one that transcends yet includes the former life. Although I died to my prior self, I was reborn again into new levels of consciousness and awareness. The new way I view the world has altered my goals, my family dynamic, my friendships, how I spend my time. I actually "see" the world differently. Other specific areas of my life show the imprint of the descent of Inanna as well.

For example, my time patiently but painfully hanging on Ereshkigal's peg significantly affected my emotional health. I can paint my experience of the world with an expanded range of emotions that before were outside both the range of my awareness and ownership.

As with my expanded range of emotions, Inanna's descent patterned for me an expanded range of human experience. During my time in the underworld I was shaken to my core. The inner securities of my personality and psyche ran screaming for higher ground, leaving me to fend helplessly for myself. As Inanna was aided by two helpers, I too was pulled from the underground by two empathic witnesses. Their compassion and experience got me up on solid ground where I continued the transformation process initiated below.

Once I had emerged shakily from the underground with uncertain steps like a toddler's, my eyes focused more acutely on the suffering in the planet and all of its inhabitants. The empathy ran deep. The tears for others flowed freely, unleashed by my own dark experiences of the unknown realms. I think of this too as a gift of Ereshkigal. She may be unrelenting in her quest as Queen of the Dead, but like a mother who knows what's best for you, she continues until the transformation is complete to her satisfaction.

As the patterns and themes from the story of Inanna continue to surface in my awareness, I know this myth now as a part of the fabric of my life. Inanna and her energies are acknowledging me in many ways today. This week I have been dreaming of lions, the animals that pulled Inanna's chariot. Glorious new spring bulbs just opened in my front yard; I learned they are called Lion's Head. In the middle of writing this I received from the Ereshkigal in my life an email containing still more crystal clear parallels to the themes discussed here.

It is evident that an ancient myth such as the the descent of Inanna, found on clay tablets over 3,500 years old, can provide insight, guidance and new clarity to help broaden the personal into the universal. This, for me, is now an experiential reality. I am inside a much bigger story. And it all started with Inanna's descent.

Seized by Odin

It took me a long time to realize my myth, or became conscious of it, but when I did I felt as if everything fell into place. My life made sense in a way that I had never felt before.

It is my strong belief that I am living within the myth of Odin, the creator and warrior god, but also a storyteller and protector of poets. When studying to get my Bachelor of Arts degree I took a few courses that dealt with personal mythology and one course actually called Personal Myth, but during the years of trying to understand my own myth, I never felt like I made any worthwhile progress.

It was not until I wrote my Master's Thesis in Depth Psychology that I finally realized my personal myth. To write my thesis I had to write about my background as an atheist, born and raised in Sweden, into a family where religion has always been shunned, but where fairytales have been given much time and importance. Both my mother and my grandmother used to tell me stories and read fairytales to me, and as I grew up I became a storyteller myself.

Living the myth of Odin began as I was born into a geographical region steeped in Norse mythology. For my first eighteen years I lived in a village called Valla, and the village center was called Valhalla, a village with roots from the 11th century. I was born on a Wednesday, the day of Odin (Wotan).

As a child I always mythologized natural wonders, such as the rain and thunder, which weren't just rain and thunder, but Thor who rode across the sky in his chariot while fighting giants. From his hammer came the thunder, and the lightning was his chariot racing across the sky. Then, when I was out of high school, my first real job was as a tour guide in a church in my home town. The church had lots of history behind it and I could go on for hours talking about it and telling stories to people who came by.

Eventually I moved to California to attend graduate school, and after many years of studying different subjects, such as humanistic psychology, biopsychology, and abnormal psychology to find out what I was interested in, I eventually took a Jungian-based psychology course, and then another and another.

Growing tired of Greek mythology, and of my feelings being disconnected from my ancestral roots, I decided to focus in on Norse mythology and ended up writing a thesis about how Norse myths changed as Christianity arrived in Scandinavia.

When reading up on Odin, a few things tipped me off about my myth. First, Odin created the world and the humans within it and, being seized by his myth, I attempted to create a map of the progress of Norse myths throughout the Christian era, moving from being gods to becoming fairytale creatures. Second, Odin was able to go back and forth between the upper and lower worlds like a shaman or a magician. To my family and friends, this is what I do. To write my thesis I looked at the collective unconscious of culture and village through mythology and folklore and brought to consciousness my findings. Third, Odin sacrificed his left eye in the well of Mimir to gain wisdom, and with this eye he tends to the world of the unconscious, the world of myth and magic, while with his healthy eye tends to consciousness, the everyday world. I was born with a defect on my left eye that causes my pupil to be much larger than normal and unable to contract in bright light, making me unconsciously always close this eye when outside or when it's too bright. Hence, me left eye works better in the dark, or in dim lighting. Mythically, one can say that with this eye I tend to the world of the unconscious, while with my regular eye I tend to consciousness. Fourth, of all the Norse gods, Odin was the storyteller, and in a sense the creator of poetry and writing. I am attempting to tell the story underlying Norse fairytales, the story behind the story.

This last connection to Odin was reinforced by a vision quest undertaken by my Master's cohort, during which I walked up on top of a mountain, or large hill, overlooking a huge valley. There I stood pondering what the meaning of all this was, what the meaning of writing my thesis was, as well as my life as a whole. After hours of standing meditation, I realized I must have looked like a priest, cloaked in blue like Odin. In the days before this vision quest my cohort had actually called me a "priest" twice, and then once again right after the quest.

From having had no clue about what I wanted to do with my life, I feel at ease now, knowing that I will always be the storyteller and that my life will always revolve around trying to bring the unconscious to consciousness through storytelling and adventures in folklore and folk beliefs.

When I was forced to become the traveler again, having to move back to Sweden after being declined a work visa in the US, this seeming setback reconnected me with my ancestral roots. It will also be much easier to follow my true passion of Norse mythology and folklore from over here and to write my own books on the topic. Then I will truly have to create maps linking the past and the present and the psychological aspects of folklore with literal history.

The Transformation of Cassandra

We never know when an offhand remark will change the course of one's life. One day in class I casually mentioned that I have often felt that my middle name should be Cassandra, the unfortunate prophetess who foretold the fall of Troy but who was not believed. I felt that my words, like hers, felled on deaf ears. To my surprise my comment was taken seriously and I was encouraged to research the Cassandra myth.

During this process I discovered that if we are fortunate, there comes a time when we recognize that the stories we tell ourselves are precisely that—stories that combine enough truth with fiction to pass for fact. Using the technique of indwelling [a heuristic research method similar to Jungian "active imagination"—CC], I invited the Cassandra energy to speak to me via paper and pen. She told me of her history and of events that led up to the destruction of Troy, and as she did she passed along many lessons. Since I recognized her as a kindred spirit, I called her Cousin Cassandra (I am Cousin Ann). This was her challenge to me:

"To change the course of one's life requires the strength to do what is difficult, and it is unwise to think that someone else can do it for you. Do you hear the lesson behind the story? You and you alone must do the work to move the mountains where your dreams are buried.

"Now Cousin Ann, it is your turn to inform me. Return to the memories buried in the past but not forgotten. Reread your journals, your poetry and your dreams. Breathe in the living past to revive the present that appears dead. Go back in time to recall that moment when you dared not say what you were thinking. Recall the other moments in your life when you sacrificed your feelings and gave them no words. See how long have you been self-censoring, self-silencing your speech and spirit?"

I did as she requested and began to see the origin and power of my personal myth and its influence in shaping how I perceived myself, my life, and others.

The Cassandra myth teaches me that while others may choose to ignore or invalidate what I have to say, it is more important for me to believe in myself and to speak up. During times when I backslide into silence and self-doubt, I find it helpful to return to paper and pen to allow Cassandra-within to counsel me.

Paradoxically, the tragedy of the myth transformed when I chose to embrace and embody it. It became an inspiration for personal empowerment and growth by being a means for exploring the interiority of my being, the stories I tell myself, and the interpretation I give to life events. To this day, Cousin Cassandra continues to be my ally as I step up to new career challenges and opportunities.

Percival's Quest

While working on my master's thesis, which seeks to discover ways of sensing into and relating with the subtle energetic interconnections between human and other life forms on Earth, my thesis advisor suggested that I identify my personal myth, stating that by doing so I would perhaps find the language I needed to convey my thoughts and experiences.

When he suggested this, I felt overwhelmed. For one thing, I had a limited education when it came to myths: I only knew the most commonly told Greek and Roman myths. For another, I didn't know how to go about identifying my personal myth, and didn't really know what questions to ask, how to ask them, or whom to ask. So after a brief search on the Web that yielded nothing but multiple and imprecise results, I gave up the active search. In a casual but sincere way, I surrendered this search to the Universe, requesting that if a personal myth would serve me or the thesis process, that I be led to that myth.

A few months passed. One evening I was having a conversation with one of my professors at the university. I mentioned to him that I had this "open question" as to what is my personal myth. He suggested that I check out the Knights of the Round Table that are a part of the King Arthur myths, suggesting that I might find my myth among this group of characters. I found the idea intriguing for some reason, and decided that I would do that.

The next day, I mentioned this idea to my thesis advisor. He responded with enthusiasm, telling me that the quest for the Holy Grail represents a quest for the Divine Feminine and a reconnection of human individuals and society to the Earth. He suggested I look at the knight Perceval. When I was first inquiring into my personal myth a few months before, a friend whose knowledge of myths exceeded my own had mentioned this knight as well, but I wasn't receptive to the idea at that time. Now my body vibrated in excitement and recognition. I sensed that this was right, that Perceval was a myth that was operating through my life at this time, and I felt a joy of recognition.

Serendipitously, my advisor happened to know an expert in Grail mythology and put me in contact with her. With her help, I was able to find resources to help me explore this myth. What I in fact did was create an independent study focusing on the quest for the Holy Grail, and spent eleven weeks reading and researching these myths. This was a rich and rewarding experience, and the myth of Perceval (especially as related by 12th century author Wolfram von Eschenbach, who wrote the epic classic *Parzival*), seemed to resonate with my own history and current life journey. However, I could not have guessed the ways that I would *somatically* experience elements of this myth, as I did in the following account from my independent study, completed June 13, 2008:

For the third year in a row, I had been participating in a process that put me in touch with primary energies flowing in our bodies and connecting with the flow of life energy throughout all beings on the Earth, work called Holistic Sexuality. During a week-long retreat in which I was doing this work in a focused manner, I had been feeling pain in the area between my genitals and my belly button, an area called the Vital Center. It is in this center that Life emerges in humans and connects us to the dynamic rhythms of the Earth. It was not a severe pain, but an ache that would arise from time to time.

On the second day of the workshop, the pain intensified. I also felt as if poison was filling my body, and I felt nauseous. When I spoke with my practice partner, I told him without quite knowing what I said that I felt as if a spear had pierced my Vital Center. As with the Fisher King, the wound was gaping and festering. The pain that filled me was emotional or psychic as well as physical; I also knew that the pain was not mine alone.

I left my partner and sought comfort outside. I lay down on a towel and asked the ground to support me, perhaps relieve some of the discomfort. The pain eased for moments at a time, but the nausea did not abate. I finally got up and walked to my cabin, wondering if I had caught some kind of flu. Once in the cabin, I tried to vomit but couldn't.

I walked into the solitude of my bedroom, and soon began sobbing. The sobs were wracking sobs, as if my body were being turned inside out. The pain eased significantly by the next day, though I was cognizant of some trace of its presence.

> On the last full day of the retreat, I decided to walk in the river. I had done it the year before, and found it to be a rich and magical experience. This year, however, I could not relax into the walk. The river was deeper and colder than the previous year, and I found myself unable to sink into—to surrender to—the river or into the experience. I actually walked on tiptoes through part of the journey, not willing to let my abdomen experience the cold. I felt unsettled by the walk, angry and weak, incompetent as a man, a failure.
>
> The next morning I awoke and felt as if the spear had pierced my heart. I sensed the River calling to me again, enticing me to immerse myself. I couldn't, and I sought to forgive myself for this "failure" of courage. The River called again, saying I could walk along it rather than in it. Reluctantly, I got up and walked to the river. I felt the Land speak to me of my failure and inadequacy, saying "Yes, bring that along!" Though the task was too big for me, beyond my capabilities, the Land seemed to say, "I want you to do it, even though you may fail." At one point I got angry and roared. After this I felt the River ask me to offer it my heart. I opened myself to the River, and it was as if I could feel the cold water rushing through my heart.
>
> I remembered then that I had with me a red heart-shaped rock I had brought to the retreat. In a ritualistic gesture, I threw the rock into the river.

I am still considering the lessons of this experience, but turning to another portrayal of the myth of Perceval and the Quest for the Holy Grail helped me hold what had happened. As I wrote in the final paper for my independent study:

> I am reminded of a wonderful scene in the 1981 movie *Excalibur* [dir. John Boorman]. After failing to obtain the Grail and then being hanged from a tree, Perceval is driven into a nearby river. Nearly drowning, Perceval pulls off all his armor and emerges from the river nearly naked...The combined failures, accompanied by his near-death hanging experience and the "baptism/initiation" in the river, strips Perceval of inner or outer trappings that belonged to a self too small to receive the Grail. Dripping wet and nearly naked, Perceval is given another chance to retrieve the Grail, which he is now able to do.

Encountering and living this story invites me into a deepen connection to my own character and power, calling me to relate more closely to the powers of the beings and lands around me as I engage more deeply the work that I am called to do. As I move forward, I will continue to hold Perceval and the Quest as key reference points, returning again and again to the stories and images that emerge, in the variety of forms available to us today, from these myths.

Sedna

Samhain Celebration, San Francisco 2007:

In the center of the room a group of women are dressed and masked as various Goddesses. They carry mirrors and sing, "You are the Goddess!" My friend and I take turns identifying many of the Goddesses. One catches my eye. She is ghastly and pale, she has no hands, one side of her face is skeletal. She sways and undulates as though she were underwater. I can't take my eyes off her. There is something familiar about her. I can't identify her and I can't stop looking at her. Who is she?

She is Sedna, the Inuit Goddess who is betrayed and killed by her father. When he throws her out of his kayak out of fear for his life, she swims back and holds onto one side. Terrified, he takes out his hunting knife and cuts off her fingers and hands. As the fingers fall into the sea they become the animals the Inuit depend on for their daily nourishment: whales, seals, and fishes.

Sedna sinks to the bottom of the ocean and lives in a house of bones. All the broken taboos and sins against children, women and nature fall through the sea and onto Sedna. When the accumulation becomes too much, she sobs in pain. The sea creatures gather around her to comfort her. This creates a time of scarcity for the Inuit people, and they petition the shaman for help. The shaman purifies himself for the dangerous journey to the underwater world where Sedna lives. He sings to Sedna, combs her hair and cleanses her body. She is soothed and comforted by his song. The sea creatures return to the Inuit and Sedna's sobs are no longer heard in the ocean waves.

The psychic pull I felt toward Sedna was a result of a similar story line in my life. Growing up in a home where the father held omnipotent power over the family, a home where the feminine was repressed and diminished, meant that my hands were symbolically cut off. When I was seventeen, in the midst of the Women's Movement of the Sixties, my father threatened my life by holding a gun to my head after I questioned his authority and the limited role of women in my home and in the world.

Sedna's arrival and my recognition of her sent me deep into the watery underworld. I cried for two months. During this time I dreamed of a deep wound being lanced, with blood and pus pouring out of it. I cried for my own feminine wounding and for the collective wounding. I cried for the destruction of the Earth and her children. I cried for the dead zones in the ocean, for the animals that have become extinct, for the clearcut forests and the mining activity that cuts into the Mother with no regard for the ecological damage being done. I cried for the disconnection I felt as a woman from the masculine. I felt myself to be conduit for the release of the deeply held grief within the Earth herself. One morning I dreamed that my circulatory system and the Earth's were the same.

This intense and cathartic period was supported within my psyche by the arrival of a male ally (like the shaman in the Sedna myth) who showed up in my dream, advising me to allow myself to dissolve into my grief. I was comforted by his words. Soon after this I dreamed of the deep wound being sutured closed.

I then began to have dreams that contained a circular theme. In one, I was gardening. My garden was circular and well watered, so I turned off the water. In another, I explored a new development of circular houses and received a new name: Solhestia.

Hestia is the first born child to Rhea and Cronos and the last one to be freed from her fathers' bowels after he swallowed his children out of fear. Her symbol is the circle, like the first hearths and the temples built to honor her. She is the ancient hearth fire of the clan mothers, a place of sustenance, spiritual renewal, community and warmth. She is the least known of the Olympians; there are few images of her, but as an important presence in the home or temple, she is the living flame in the center. No home or temple was considered sanctified until Hestia arrived. The Romans called her Vesta.

She was anonymous but at the same time greatly honored. Each Greek city-state had a common fire and every colony took this sacred fire with them from the home city to light the new fire in the colony. A newly married couple would light their new hearth with fire from the family hearth. In this way Hestia represents continuity, interrelatedness and community. The essence of Hestia is the living flame within each of us that unites us all as a common family.

Hestia's entrance is more difficult to pinpoint. I suspect she has been with me for a long time, unacknowledged and quietly keeping balance in a childhood full of drama and conflict. I was not conscious of her in my life until my work with Sedna. The emotional depths I reached in working with Sedna along with the purging of the pain around the feminine made it possible for me to acknowledge my serene, calm center. In the emotional storm of Sedna I found the calm center, the still point of Hestia. [I suspect that Sedna and Hestia are parallel goddesses: two faces worn by one archetypal power. —CC]

My life story contains the pain and suffering of Sedna's mythology, but it also contains the warmth and spiritual depth one can reach through suffering and healing deep pain. Like Hestia, I was swallowed by the father and had to find my way out of the darkness. As a result of this wound I was propelled onto a spiritual path at a young age in an effort to contain the pain and confusion.

I now hold a central and honored place with in my small family. My daughters, sons-in-law, and grandchildren give my life an emotional richness that no outer manifestation or accomplishment could provide or replace. I am happiest when I can stay home, spending my time with artistic projects or puttering around my house. I have a rich inner life and find restoration in solitude.

How to Be a Champion: Joan of Arc (by Lola McCrary)

Had I been able to sit down and chose a personal myth with full deliberation and reflection, it probably would not have been that of a possibly mentally ill, non-literate teenager, who against all the conventions of her society spoke truth to authority, donned armor in defense of her king and country and—after three years of successful effort and integrity—was betrayed to the enemy by the same king, who stood by while her enemies, using her church and religion as cover, executed her on trumped-up heresy charges by burning her at the stake.

In the 15th century C.E., for goodness' sake. Six hundred years ago.

I was raised a Roman Catholic, so I knew from a very young age that Joan of Arc was my patron saint. I had the same middle name as my mother: Jeanne, the French spelling of Joan. I read lots of lives of the saints—including Joan's—when I was young. But while I knew the story, I had no conscious relationship to it other than interest in reading about my patron saint. That is, until late summer, 2007.

I turned fifty years old that year. I had been twenty-five years away from the Roman Catholic Church, even after getting a degree in religious studies from a Roman Catholic college. My time away from Christianity included involvement with atheism, neo-paganism, Ken Wilber's Integral Model, some academic study of depth psychology, and lots of personal therapy. By way of an intense spiritual experience the previous year, I had gone (in the course of about ten minutes) from being agnostic about the possibility of a personal relationship with God, to the beginning of a mystical awareness that has continued to grow. By August, 2007, I was in another round of thinking that I had it more or less together.

That summer I was in class with Craig at JFK University, fascinated by the material on myths and archetypes but not sure how it all related to my life. A mention of my name came up. I had considered my name in the past in connection with myth and archetypes, but this time I felt like a ton of bricks had fallen on me. Every cell in my body lit up. It was like I was watching many pieces of an unfinished jigsaw puzzle get put in their proper places right in front of my eyes. I would give almost anything for a picture of the look on my face at that moment. Correspondences between myself and Joan moved into view and sat there, patiently waiting for acknowledgement. I started madly typing notes about what occurred to me in those first moments of awareness.

Here are a couple of those correspondences:

When I chose a martial art for myself I selected aikido, which is a cooperative, defensive art. Joan (despite the way she is portrayed in movies, plays and computer games) led her king's armies bearing her own standard so that she would not have to participate in the worst of the fighting. She told the inquisitors at her trial that—as instructed by her voices—she had never killed anyone.

When Joan faced the church leaders after her capture, she was condemned falsely not only because her individual awareness of God through her voices and visions was too threatening to the mix of church and state that existed at that time, but because those voices had proven true. The primary reason I left the Roman Catholic church in 1982 was because I felt that my voice—as a woman and a liberal—had no place in John Paul II's church. The service I most wanted to embody, that of being a priest, was unacceptable because I was born female. I left before I could be rejected—a choice not open to Joan in 1431. In retrospect I now feel that even then I was changing my personal myth. In our day and age (and despite the Roman Catholic Church's continued efforts), no one should be silenced just because they question the orthodox teachings.

Coincidence, some might say. Too much time listening to someone who had made describing those connections part of his life work. Wishful thinking. An overblown sense of my own destiny. Perhaps. But we are meaning making creatures, and even if I am making this meaning up, the results of working consciously with the myth of Joan of Arc have been nothing but positive. I believe, however, that personal myth is considerably more than that.

Where do the typologies in our life come from? Did I make deliberate choices about what kind of a life I wanted to live before I was born—what kind of a person I wanted to be? Do I simply assign meaning to the complexities of life as they occur, as I am best able in any given moment? How many coincidences does it take to equal Jungian synchronicity? If those synchronicities take on a pattern, am I shaping them into a personal myth because it makes me feel better? Is it a valid form of meaning making? Does any of this really matter, especially when much of our human community lives in want and with suffering? Does it matter when that same human community is allowing its home to die?

These are the questions I have been considering since Joan stepped out of my personal shadow into glorious consciousness. In all aspects of personal growth and meaning-making, self-delusion and inflation of self-image are an ever present danger. Why, I asked myself, is it important to me that I identify with Joan? What result is this having on my life? Is it truly a positive result?

One nearly immediate result of conscious awareness of my personal myth was that I got my Christianity back. In November of 2007 I renewed my baptismal and confirmation vows in a "heretical" Old Catholic (not Roman Catholic) ceremony. The presider at the Eucharist was a woman. The deacon and bishop involved are openly non-heterosexual. I found a Christian community where my voice is accorded respect, where personal experience is examined with an assumption of validity, and where accidents of birth (such as gender and sexual orientation) are not a ban to service.

Another positive outcome of acknowledging Joan's myth in my life has been that I more consciously decide what, or who, I want to champion. That way I am not wasting time and energy in places I am not needed, wanted or appreciated. And I've allowed myself to become the most important person I champion as I walk the hero's journey towards greater self-knowledge and service.

As the stories above demonstrate, we live in a time when many ways of knowing are surfacing, some privately held, others attracting worldwide attention. No single way, whether that of religion, science, or some feudal lord, will ever dominate again. Whether he knows it yet or not, proud Procrustes has been dethroned.

Feel free, therefore, to trust the experiential "aha" that tells you by lighting up your mind and body: This myth is true for me. If it begins as a fleeting intuition, it will need plenty of substantiating, but in the end it must fit for you beyond any consideration of "proof" or claim. When the knowing in the mind and gut locks in and grabs you firmly and inescapably, you will recognize the myth as it stares into your eyes. Then the next stage can begin: learning to live with your myth.

CHAPTER 5
Rebecca's Story

I was a self-described corporate survivor, having worked in corporate America for fifteen years, before bravely enrolling in graduate school to find myself, on the very first day, in a class called Paradigms of Consciousness. One of the first assignments was to write one to two pages of our "personal myth." I wondered, "Personal myth? What's that?"

As the instructor patiently described the assignment and reassured the students we would not be given a letter grade for our papers, I was still in a quandary. In retrospect, I believe it was part of the process to look inside and begin the journey of self-reflection, introspection, and self-discovery by interpreting the assignment with the best understanding I had at the time. After being in a career where I produced pages of reports, prepared countless presentations, and authored plans and strategies, it was all I could do to write a one page account of my own mythical story. I had never before given much thought to who I was. Not really.

In the course in Archetypal Mythology personal myth was revisited, and we were tasked to uncover, from a depth-psychological perspective, the storied life we came into the world with, identifying themes that kept replaying. After having flailed a bit at my first attempt in the earlier class, I eagerly took up the challenge of digging deeper.

Finding My Story

I started by taking an inventory of my life and wrote a narrative. I looked at the types of relationships I had with family, relatives, friends, and significant intimates from childhood all the way through adulthood. I paid attention to the types of activities I engaged in and the types of things I was attracted to. Likewise, I noted what I didn't like. I looked at the types of jobs I took and what I did in those jobs; what I studied in college and why.

I wanted to understand what mattered to me most, and what formed the basis for the decisions I made in life. Now I had something to reflect upon before I started researching age-old stories.

The Meaning of "Rebecca"

The easiest place to start finding my myth was to look into the origins and meaning of my name, Rebecca.

I found a definition of "Rebecca": "to bind." I then looked up "to bind." The definition that made sense within the context of my life was, "to form a link or relationship based on loyalty, affection, or a shared experience." Another meaning I found for Rebecca was the term "captivating": "attracting and holding somebody's attention by charm or other pleasing features." I thought about my former modeling career.

Further investigation revealed other meanings, such as "to snare" and "to noose." I found the definition of "snare" to mean, "to entrap by alluring deception," and the definition of noose to mean, "something that traps somebody in an unpleasant or unwanted situation." A further interpretation suggested that Rebecca's beauty was used to trap men.

When looking at all the meanings from a bird's eye view, the common thread was bringing together and making a connection or forming a relationship, whether it was through attraction or strategic means. The goal was the same regardless of the tactic.

The Story of Rebekah

The next step was to find out about the story that held my name.

I found out that Rebekah was a character in the Hebrew scriptures. She was described as a maiden of beauty, modesty, and kindness. She was known to be positive, energetic, and ambitious. She exuded confidence, bravery, and resourcefulness, impressing people who met her. The actions in her life suggest she was an active planner and doer.

In her story, Abraham's servant, who was sent away to find a wife for Abraham's son Isaac, meets her at a well. She kindly offers water for him and his camels. The servant is attracted to her beauty and kindness, and decides she is a suitable bride for Isaac. Rebekah is asked if she would like to become Isaac's wife, which set a precedent. She agrees. Isaac meets her and it is love at first sight for both of them.

Isaac had a deep bond with his mother Sarah. Sarah was very old at the time he married Rebekah. When Sarah died, the deep bond Isaac had with his mother was replaced with his love for Rebekah.

Rebekah was barren for twenty years before conceiving the twins Esau and Jacob. The boys were fraternal twins and very different from each other. Esau was described as popular, strong, earthy, and carefree. Jacob was described as the intelligent sibling. Since Esau was the eldest, it was his birthright to receive the blessing and primary inheritance. The blessing allowed legal power to govern the tribe. Isaac favored Esau because he was a hunter and brought venison. Rebekah favored Jacob, and loved him joyfully without any qualifications or reservations.

When Isaac's eyesight failed as he found himself near death, he knew it was time to make his blessing. He was ready to pass it on to his eldest son. However, Rebekah did not think Esau was suitable to govern the tribe. She felt Jacob would be able to make decisions for the tribe based on wisdom rather than emotion and impulse. She devised a plan with Jacob to deceive Isaac into believing Jacob was Esau. She dressed Jacob in Esau's clothing and had him put on kid gloves to feel like Esau's skin. So the blessing and major part of inheritance was passed onto Jacob. At a time when the world was unpredictable and possibly dangerous, her cunning was admired as a means of survival for her family and the tribe.

Naturally Esau became enraged when the deception was discovered. He vowed to kill Jacob once his father passed away. Rebekah heard what Esau was going to do. She once again employed her farsightedness and shrewdness and had Jacob sent away to live with her family. This became a sacrifice she had to make to save the life of her son, as Jacob never returned before her death.

Rebekah as Metaphor

This story shows up as a metaphor in my life in several ways. I was encouraged early in my life to make decisions on my own and was actively supported by my family. Like her, I gave birth to fraternal twins late in childbearing years.

Her story of unconditional love she gives to her son mirrors the type of love I hold for others. Reciprocated love is magnificent, but giving love unconditionally has a magic all of its own. The following quote by an unknown author resonates strongly with me: "Love is all we need. We learn throughout our lives, but we are only truly alive when we are able to love."

Rebekah employs shrewdness as a means to an end. In general, if it is for the greater good, or if it is for love, I would agree with her that this is a workable strategy. She showed self-sacrifice for the love of her son, not merely for emotional martyrdom. I can identify with her character and motivation. She thinks things through and utilizes her strengths to the best of her ability. I try to do the same.

In her life there was much separation, and her innate purpose, also reflected in her name, was to bring together, "to bind," as she does when she marries Isaac. She gives him a way to reconcile himself to the loss of his mother by becoming the woman he loves after Sarah dies. She creates a family. She intelligently keeps the cohesiveness of the tribe by ensuring the best leader takes over to govern. All in all, Rebekah's story remains one of connection, creation, and relationship.

Although much meaning came from researching my name, I did not feel like the story was complete. I sensed there was more to find out. My next exploration was among the Greek pantheon.

Searching the Greek Pantheon

I began reading stories of the Greek goddesses in books and on the Internet, looking for clues of which myth might resonate with me. I saw bits and pieces of who I was in many of them. I sought to match profiles against mine, pulling life experience examples in my mind to identify the closest fit. A few examples of the screening process include the Greek goddesses Artemis, Athena, and Demeter.

I could identify with the competitive fierceness of Artemis. Certainly, in this day and age, it is admirable to be a fully empowered, independent woman. I felt I had competed well in the corporate arena. What I didn't identify with was the tendency of Artemis to have what I perceived as an overt feminist leaning. Although I value and believe in equality for women, I do so in other ways, more subtly.

Then there was Athena, with her many gifts of wisdom. I consider myself a lifelong learner and observer of the world serious about honing my practicality, objectivity, confidence, and ambition. Athena was also a goddess of crafts, and as a child I loved to create and appreciate art of many kinds. However, Athena women are very rationalistic, favoring sensibility over the emotional cues that guide flows of information. They tend to be ruled by logic, with their heads commanding their hearts. I have a definite proclivity toward ways of knowing rooted in my emotional life.

Demeter is the archetypal mother. As the mother of twins, whom I would protect and defend with all my might, I wondered if perhaps Demeter offered a mythological template for my life. Demeter was a very nurturing goddess and helpful to others. But her empathic nature goes with being a caretaker: my first red flag that this wasn't me. Also, Demeter was vulnerable to men, whereas my experience had been of being protected by them, not victimized. I kept reading and researching, attempting to find a tale, a narrative, a characterization that reflected my own schema for organizing events, dreams, motifs, relationships, meaningful coincidences...

When I found the right myth, I immediately resonated with her characterization and outlook on life. She viewed the world through the same lens I did. As I read more about her stories, passions, disposition, and reactions, I knew I had found the primary likeness to my experience. The mythological image was Aphrodite, the goddess of love, beauty, joy, pleasure, and procreation. The Romans thought of her as Venus. This discovery complemented the findings in the story of Rebekah, and began to fill in a larger composite picture of my personal myth.

Aphrodite

As I sorted her stories for metaphors and deeper meanings, and the psychological parallels on and below the surface, I noted the tales that conveyed the strongest identifiable parallels. Exploring this archetypal image and its fit was fascinating, revealing, and unnerving all at the same time, because it was like looking in a mirror where you cannot ignore the image reflected in all its mysterious magnificence and brutally honest imperfection.

There are two versions of her beginning. Homer tells of her being conceived through the physical attraction between Zeus and earth goddess Dionne. In the more violent version from Hesiod, she is said to have risen from the foam in the sea stirred when Chronus tossed into the sea the severed genitals of this father, the sky god Uranus. In this version she emerges from the sea as a fully-grown goddess. When I was a child, I always had a sense that I was already a grown-up inside. I couldn't wait to become an adult.

One of Aphrodite's gifts was a type of attractiveness that drew people toward her. At a young age I found that boys were drawn to me. Zeus was fearful of the feuds that might start as a result of competing suitors for Aphrodite, so in one version of the myth, he had her married off to Hephaestus, the Olympian god of metalworking, masonry, and sculpture.

Hephaestus had been known to manufacture works of exquisite craftsmanship. He had also been born with crippled feet or became that way when ejected from Olympus. The man I married is an engineer by education and has had a long career in the manufacture of leading-edge technologies. In his young adult life his back was injured, causing chronic pressure on his left foot. As for the union of

Aphrodite and Hephaestus, it was said that craftsmanship wedded to beauty created art. Both my grade-school-aged twins have identified themselves as artists. They both love exploring art in many types of mediums.

As one of the oldest goddesses, Aphrodite took part in many Olympian stories. She is an alchemical goddess by virtue of how she brings together elements for their transformation. This alchemical nature also finds itself mirrored in Rebekah's story and name.

Common throughout Aphrodite's stories was her need to bring love into the lives of others, and to know love in her own life. Aphrodite was at her best when she exemplified the force of attraction and passionate connection. Her notable relationships included Ares the god of war, Hermes the messenger god, and Adonis, a life-death-rebirth deity. Reading about these gods uncovered striking archetypal similarities between them and significant men in my life.

Aphrodite's Shadow

Without awareness of one's myth, its shadow side, which also seeks expression, can surface surreptitiously. One way to know your myth has you by the throat is when it keeps playing out literally, as was the case of Marilyn Monroe, who found herself locked into the aphroditic role of a love and sex goddess, to her undoing. I discovered the many ways I get caught in my version of the myth when reflecting on how I react in different situations. Aphrodite became cold, angry, and vengeful when her gifts were not honored. In one story she was unimpressed with a woman's heartlessness, so she turned her to stone.

I've been known to "clam up" when someone doesn't respond the way I hope, as Aphrodite felt when a young sea-god refused to accompany her to Olympus and she turned him into a shellfish. She was a free spirit who could not be controlled. This shows up in me through putting things off in order to enjoy and smell the flowers and through playing and having fun as a temporary escape from problems.

Another way I find myself getting caught in the myth is when I take things at face value without looking below the surface. This is a component of Aphrodite's trusting nature and of her capacity to appreciate life's little details. Materialism is also a big shadow for her, as represented also by the Roman goddess Venus, who sometimes feels she can't do without the illusory security materialism seems to bring. Ultimately this materialist shadow is disempowering and vain and limits choices. Knowing this, one can choose to succumb to the trap or do things differently. With awareness, the locus of choice belongs to me instead of to my myth.

When embracing my myth, it was a relief to discover its limitations. Understanding the realm where Aphrodite's gifts flourished, and where some things were better left to the talents of others, allowed me to give myself permission and feel no regret for sticking to my strengths. When Aphrodite mistakenly entered the Trojan War to save her son, she got hurt in her attempt, and her son had to be rescued by Apollo. As Zeus correctly told her in the *Iliad*, "No, my child, not for you are the works of warfare. Rather concern yourself only with the lovely secrets of marriage, while all this shall be left to Athena and sudden Ares."

At a pivotal point in my career, it was essential that I obtain an advanced business degree in order to keep earning promotions. The defining question was, "Do I pursue an MBA and actively compete, or do I remain content with what I've achieved?" True to my myth, I instinctively yielded to my Athena and Artemis sisters to carry the swords and compete in head-to-head battle with the men, which they have done with amazing success. My most fulfilling career accomplishments have been in building relationships and forging collaboration for next generation project ideas. I brought design experts together and in alchemical fashion facilitated the generative fashioning of new product concepts while still within the world of business. I became a subject matter expert where others sought my input and recommendations. My strengths included the aphroditic qualities of bringing people and ideas together, offering consultative resources, and forging productive change. Learning the myth of Aphrodite was a wonderful validation that I made the right career choices for myself.

Living with My Myth

Knowledge of my myth provides a type of internal compass. As I define a new career for the second half of my life, it is much clearer what path to take and what role I will play.

I find myself increasingly drawn toward participating in the growing movement of societal response to pressing concerns about climate change, peak oil, and environmental destruction. It makes sense from a mythical perspective that I am drawn into what could be perceived as a series of conflicts because Aphrodite naturally seeks to bring opposites together. New ways to live in an energy-constrained world in the future conflict with old habits of wasteful consumption. Likewise, conflict occurs between people who want to keep things the same and those who want to change them. All this reflects a collision between what Joanna Macy identifies as the industrial growth paradigm and the emerging earth-based life-sustaining paradigm. At issue is the artificial separation of self from world.

I am passionately driven to bring people together to envision the type of future we want to live in, and to invite creative solutions for a sustainable and beautiful environment for our generation and those to come. Living in a beautiful world, visioning what could be, collaborating on projects to create our own responses to changes that lie ahead from the bottom up instead of from the top down: these goals carry energy and excitement for me. The aphroditic element makes the movement toward a new future attractive, adds soul, and stimulates the imagination and the senses. The senses, in fact, make up a real urgency of the environmental crisis. We numb ourselves to how bad things look, smell, and feel, but the ugliness breaks through. As award-winning author, educator, and environmental champion David Orr writes:

> Ugliness is, I think, the surest sign of disease, or what is now being called "unsustainability." Show me the hamburger stands, neon ticky-tacky strips leading toward every city in America, and the shopping malls, and I'll show you devastated rain forests,

> a decaying countrywide, a politically dependent population, and toxic waste dumps. It is all of a fabric.
>
> —*Ecological Literacy*, p. 88

Paying attention to our besieged senses can awaken the call to shift something within and around us.

In conclusion, it is important that the stories we live are held as metaphors to keep from literalizing them. I hold awareness of a psychic/mythic structure I can now control instead of it controlling me. Through the process of discovery, the image of Aphrodite changed into *my* version of Aphrodite, while still carrying the essence and gifts of the original. Through my work, my embodied aphroditic tendencies have also undergone transformation: what I once experienced as impulsiveness has settled into a greater sense of calm and deeper trust and confidence in myself. The strength of knowing my myth adds solid validation to knowing I'm on the right track with my life's purpose, having learned over the years that tending what is most meaningful to me of itself exerts its influence around me.

CHAPTER 6

Living Your Myth

It's amazing and even stunning, this power of old stories to hang on. We even talk about consciousness as a substance that endures, with more of it automatically considered a very good thing. Idealists now speak of "conscious capitalism," "conscious politics," and "conscious romance," as though these could shed their roots in deep unconsciousness.

In living one's myth, however, it's not really a question of more consciousness. Both Freud and Steinbeck had a fairly accurate idea of their personal myth, but both continued to run painfully up against the edge of its stage nonetheless. Yet Jung, who for years did not suspect how faithfully he was Faust, lived his myth well and successfully turned its tale toward vistas wide and deep. What's the difference?

More Consciousness—or Freer Imagination?

In San Francisco, the city named after the joyfully idealistic and dionysian St. Francis, a homeless man by the name of Mark Bittner began feeding and caring for wild cherry-headed parrots who descended from the air to enjoy in his company. After a time he became such an expert on them that he and they caught the attention of filmmaker Judy Irving. In *The Wild Parrots of Telegraph Hill*,

Irving unknowingly strikes a mythically tinged historic note by asking Bittner why he wears his hair so long. Because, he explains, he hasn't met anyone yet to cut it for. Toward the end of the film he lets her do it. Yet when St. Francis first met St. Clare, saint of projected images, he cut *her* hair off, nor were they able to consummate their relationship. Why did this San Franciscan recurrence of the story of Francis and Clare turn out differently? More specifically, how did the tale of an unrequited love come full circle and find such beautiful closure even though neither Irving nor Bittner were aware of being caught up in that tale?

Ultimately, knowing one's myth is less important than being true to it. By following their fascinations—caring for birds, making films—Bittner and Irving did what the story required of them without fully comprehending what it was. They were being what the ancient Greeks would have called *eudaimonic:* in good standing with the inner call, even when it asked things of them that pushed beyond the rational or the sensible. The call isn't interested in common sense or in agendas for higher realization. It's interested in myth-making, in realizing and re-dreaming itself through human agency. To some extent it will even work to safeguard the person attempting to bear its demands. Knowing what they are makes meeting them easier, but meeting them is what evolves them and moves them and their plot line forward.

Living one's myth faithfully requires a knack for feeling into story, fantasy, and metaphor, which means preserving an intact imagination. It is no accident that the industrialized societies whose money-driven educational systems throttle fantasy are also the ones that lack a coherent mythology. One can meditate, read, therapize, and self-analyze daily and by doing so acquire a great deal of fantasy-stripped consciousness, but without a capacity for feeling into motifs and images on their own fantastic terms, the accumulated skills remain disconnected from the intrinsic sense of vocation, of being called and tasked by something beyond the personal or the egoic. (Some seekers end up so devoid of the capacity for entertaining images that they boast about no longer dreaming.)

Not the amount or degree of consciousness, then, but its color and richness help us most to come to terms with the story we are in. Imaginative living and being are less head-started than heart-based. To the eye of myth, the heart is neither a mechanical chest pump nor a chakra to bypass on the way to somewhere else. It is the seat of soulfulness and the chamber of images where extraversion and introversion pulse back and forth. The imagining heart keeps the personal myth connected to inner and outer nature while embodying its emotional potential. A story means little unless it engages one's feelings fully. The thumping heart announces it: *You're involved.*

That ear in the chest is also the primary organ of *response* (from a word meaning "to pledge"). A personal myth is nothing if not a call to respond.

The Basic Choice: Dysdaimonia or Eudaimonia

When our response to the myth and its call is passivity, we get lost in a state of *dysdaimonia*, or being out of accord with the promptings of the mythic self. This is another way of saying that we remain in a state of unconscious identification with it. This overidentification can take various forms.

For example, now and then people who learn a bit about myth excessively identify with a character not their own. One such seeker thought she was an Aphrodite even though her devilish dreams insisted otherwise. She didn't get the message because it was contrary to how she saw herself. So she kept trying to be a bright love and beauty goddess, but always through the seductive underworld maneuvers and style of dark Persephone, her true mythic self. Symptoms of an *inflationary possession* by a minor character in one's tale might include weight gain, nightmares, loss of balance, falling, flying dreams, manic moods, or other signs of lack of grounding.

Because "materialist" culture remains blind to myth, living one's personal myth unconsciously and therefore *literally* demonstrates the most common form of dysdaimonia. ("Materialist" in quotes because material is exactly what we do not love: profit, status, and possessions are ethereal strivings that serve an increasingly abstract self-image. We are dematerialists.) Literalizing one's myth acts it out without reflection. Instead of flexing psychic strength, Hercules or Cuchulainn pumps iron or joins a football team. Zeus gives up his lightning flashes of illumination for a necktie and a corner office. Osiris takes Viagra, and Isis buys it for him. Mercury trades stolen copper on the black market. Saturn administers aptly named SAT tests so the public school system can devour its children. Peter Pan jumps off the Golden Gate Bridge. Venus succumbs to vanity and painkillers.

In monotheistic cultures saturated by electronically transmitted images of Redeemers and Prophets, dysdaimonia often surfaces in an obsession with literally *saving* something or someone. Save the family. Save democracy. Save the world from bad guys; save marriage from the gays; save the public from nudity and "immorality," if not from warfare and poverty and intolerance, and least of all from hypocrisy. Collective absurdity is one sign that a mythic pull has degenerated through sheer unconsciousness into an ideological push for ever-greater control of the public.

It might seem that *psychification*, the reduction of tangible realities to psychic images, would be the opposite of literalization, but opposites can be deceiving. Literalizing insists that what can't be turned into something "practical" like a career must be irrelevant and unimportant; psychification praises the seeming irrelevancy by exalting inner work over outer action. Learn your myth but don't let it get dirty by taking it outside. Tend the inner life but don't become an activist. Splitting concrete considerations of career and relationship and how to live in the great wide world from cultivation of the imaginal life constitutes a kind of literalism-in-reverse. Taken far enough, it can reduce living one's myth as an inner-outer whole to obscure academic jargonizing of the kind that abandons the public sphere to whoever decides to dominate it. The Gnostics knew of this long ago and called it "psychism."

Joseph Campbell borrowed James Joyce's word "monomyth" to describe a heroic journey Campbell believed lay at the heart of every mythology. Without meaning to, he also left us an example of another type of dysdaimonia, *monomythologizing*: seeing things only in terms of one's myth, which in his case was a heroic one. To someone caught in an underworld myth, life is primarily about descent and disaster, whereas to a redeemer, it's all about salvation. Orpheus the charmer favors rhetoric and reverie and dislikes being tied down in any way. When persisted in, monomythologizing turns into a monotheism as other perspectives and other gods fall out of favor. To the extent we unconsciously identify with our myth, then, our myth dysdaimonically hardens into our vision-narrowing monomyth.

Dysdaimonia is rampant in part because dematerialist culture supplies so many *manic defenses* against knowing one's myth. There is the ceaseless machinery of mass distraction: people don't even have to take a walk unplugged anymore. There is the war on "negative" emotions that only drives them underground where they can grow stronger. (Have you noticed how affirmations, attaboys, and "positive thinking" can actually depress you after a while?) There is the infantile omnipotence of believing that one can do anything or go anywhere, a confusion of freedom with irresponsibility. And there is the frontier/Hollywood illusion that an old identity can be swept away to make room for one more pleasing. This often shows up as an overemphasis on changing one's myth instead of taking it on so deeply and consciously that it begins to transmute itself. Hollywood has no memory beyond abundant symptoms, inflations, and projections.

By contrast, *eudemonia*, or living in the light of one's myth, melts the iron bars of literalism, freeing the liberated soul to rejoin the breathing world. It means saying yes to your myth—and to your core self—by making its promptings and movements your own. Following out a mythic path uncritically exhibits an unconscious identification, as when the inflated General Patton, whose myth was probably Mars, insisted on becoming a literal soldier and descending to macho obnoxiousness. The eudamonic task is rather to personalize the myth, to work creatively with it so that what it wants and what you want combine to tell a fresh and vital version of the old story, completing it instead of repeating it.

Jung was a eudaimonic individual. This does not mean he was an unwounded one or even a nice man. Living your myth won't guarantee that you walk old ladies across busy roads. It won't even secure the much-lauded goal of psychic wholeness. In his worse moments Jung was an opinionated bully with bad manners. The sexual misconduct of his early midlife is well known. Yet where Faust made a deal with the devil, Jung worked actively with the shadow. Where Prometheus (the Greek Faust) was chained up on a mountain, Jung worked the "fiery magma" of his confrontation with the unconscious. Faust's obsession with progress caused the death of Philemon; Jung turned the old man into a spiritual mentor.

Eudaimonia frees the myth from playing out as before, just as it frees the individual who bears it from acting it out blindly. Saul chased Psalm-writing David into the wilderness; Thoreau, middle name of David, escorted Emerson out into it. Hildegard the Valkyrie brought heroes into Valhalla; Hildegard of Bingen, "Sybil of the Rhine" and advisor to statesmen, brought her sisters in Christ into Saint Rupertsberg. Parzival wandered in the deserts for ten long years; in Joseph Campbell's case it was five, much of it spent wandering through world literature and myth.

Although expressed above as an either-or choice, eudaimonia and dysdaimonia actually function as ideals or as poles of a continuum. No life is entirely either, and no one lives their myth in perfect wholeness. If U.S. Grant was Ulysses, he fought a successful war of reunification, but as president he did poorly at kicking corrupt suitors out of the White House: only under the second Bush administration did so many criminals in high office go unpunished. Promethean William James wore out his heart while climbing in the Adirondacks. When he died, his brother Henry recalled a persistent memory of William always being around the next corner. Even so, embracing one's myth offers a sense of purpose and meaning not available to those who only stand in its shadow.

Eudaimonia also breaks the unconscious identification that tends to monomythologize. It makes it possible to step back and ask: How am I *not* Kali or Aphrodite? What if I don't want to be an exile, don't want to follow charming Orpheus into the underworld and back to the surface? What if Zeus is my myth but I want to get off the throne for a while? How might other approaches or perspectives be useful to me now?

Because the personal myth forms the axis or template around which a life crystallizes, what is done in the service of the true or real self—the "daimon" as Hillman puts it—tends to serve the myth as well. Knowing the possibilities in the myth opens it up and allows a wider scope of response to it.

Amplifying and Personalizing Your Myth

Jung used the word "amplification" to mean researching and elaborating an image or symbol to uncover its cultural and historical parallels. Let us say a man dreams of the word "phoenix." You ask him for his associations to the word and he says, "A city in Arizona." This is important and should be pursued, but if the phoenix as a mythic image remains unexplored, the opportunity of bringing a possible unconscious death-rebirth dynamic to the surface of this dreamer's life will be lost.

Here are some ways to amplify a myth in order to come to terms with it and decide how to respond to it:

- Research the myth thoroughly. While doing so, practice thinking of its dominant plot twists and characters as metaphors and motifs: Mars as assertive power, sex as connection, incest as kinship. Note which basic themes resonate for you. Which aspects of the myth trap you? Which are fluid? Which can you make into art, song, dance, collage, film, a scrapbook, a desktop background?

- Look for prior versions of the storyline to get a sense of how the myth has wanted to evolve in the past. Film can be useful for this, especially for dealing with fears of having to live the story over literally. Patton's Mars just loves battle, but General Maximus (*Gladiator*) is an idealist. In one filmed retelling of the Arthurian cycle Lancelot makes off with Guinevere; in another Arthur dies and Lancelot and Guinevere marry; in yet another, Lancelot dies and Arthur reconciles with her. In early Welsh myth Arthur is a war chief; later, a Christian conqueror with a bad case of hubris;

still later, a bringer of peace out of war. Arthur cannot choose to do without a Guinevere, but he can choose not to marry her literally, nor does he have to die at some modern counterpart to Camlann. The tellings vary with time and place. Try to get a sense of why they vary, of what they say by varying, the potentials and twists they uncover and express. Which variations does your version require?

- Look across mythologies, pantheons, and cultures for variations of the underlying archetypes. If Deirdre feels too tragic, try Lakshmi or Aphrodite. If Aphrodite doesn't reflect enough of your fascination with the esoteric, consult Freya, who brought *seidr* (oracular knowledge) to the Aesir. For the merciful aspect of this goddess look up Kwan Yin or Saint Barbara. Beware, however, of the widespread tendency to uproot the sacred images and rites of other cultures and appropriate them for your own purposes. If those images and rites speak to your soul, then learn about the cultures that nurtured them. Don't use them to ignore your own cultural inheritances while idealizing someone else's.

In terms of personalizing the myth:

- Although the plot does not necessarily play out in the original chronological order, it can still be navigationally useful to ask: Where am I in the story? If my myth is Merlin, have I saved my mother from judgment, and if not, how did my situation turn out differently? Have I met Uther or Arthur yet? Has Nimue seduced me? How should I respond when I meet her counterpart?

- Try playing with the shadow aspect of the character you identify with most. In the spirit of what therapists call "prescribing the symptom," this can increase your consciousness of the scope of that character: which strengths are burdensome, which aspects should receive more prominence. If Aphrodite's shadow is vanity, what would it feel like to exaggerate and parody that vanity on purpose? Then go ahead and try on other roles in the story. If you tend to play the hero, what would drawing upon just a little of the outlaw or trickster be like for a change?

- Come up with a monologue for a character you tend not to favor. Even Mary Shelley's monster had a point of view, and a very eloquently stated one. How did Apollo feel when Daphne spurned him? Why does Ala, the Nigerian earth goddess, give humans a stomach ache when we break our commitments? What's behind Coyote's amazing appetite? Let them speak and find out.

- Persistent inner conflicts with outer ramifications usually take the form of a *complex:* a constellation of intense feelings and fantasies and childhood internalizations gathered around some trouble-causing central theme (Karen Horney called these themes "neurotic trends"). Your complex is exactly where your myth has you by your Achilles heel, Achilles being a patron of personal myth work. At the personal level, a complex indicates unfinished emotional business. At the mythic level, it signals where we get stuck in the story because we resist finishing the scene. It is a place of painful suspension, and trying to protect oneself through resistance strengthens the complex and hardens the myth. Usually this happens because prior pain has conditioned us to equate being true to the tale or role with having it come out badly. When Athena (or Durga or Sophia or White Buffalo Calf Woman) remains in self-betraying silence, she and those in her care suffer, but when she has spoken up in accord with her nature, china got broken. To move forward she will have to be true to herself as an assertive bringer of wisdom and culture, but in ways that do not reinjure her human host.

- Who in my life plays which parts of my myth? What parts do I play in someone else's? Very often we wind up playing all the parts of our own myth too: not only Llorona's abandoned child but the Weeping Woman in distress and maybe the absent father as well. Taking these rolls on consciously can move the story forward.

- What kind of spirituality does my myth require? What kind of relationships? If mythically I am Artemis, what intimacy I enjoy will depend on finding a balance between protective isolation and not being intruded upon.

- How does my myth connect to my vocation? What have other people with this myth made of their lives? Iacchus is often an entertainer—but is he always one? What would Mars look like as a naturalist?

- How does my myth connect me with the time I live in? How is it a response to the social forces and collective pressures flowing and cresting around and within me?

And of course, the ever-present question:

- What does my myth ask of me? What does it want?

Only you can answer that, but in terms of a general guideline, the alchemists had a helpful thought: that combining two chemicals or elements will create a reconciling Third, an alloy stronger than either alone. Living your myth means taking up the challenge to invent new mixtures and projects by combining and recombining your mortal and mythic selves. As Jung famously put it in *Archetypes and the Collective Unconscious*, "The most that we can do is dream the myth onward and give it a modern dress."

In our day this perennial task includes finding our place in a troubled yet storied world.

CHAPTER 7

Finding Your Place

It would not have surprised any of our hunting and gathering ancestors that certain myths and stories and lorescapes seem to favor certain landscapes. It surprises us because we have lost the feel for story and myth as the connective tissue which binds us to the places where we live, and because we think of those places as mindless "natural resources." If we didn't, we wouldn't permit heavy industries to dig them up, chew them up, and dump them out as waste.

For aboriginal people the natural world is soaked in story. Kiowa novelist N. Scott Momaday writes movingly about how listening to an old woman tell stories was like hearing them emanate from the land itself. Anthropologist Keith Basso talks about the Western Apache tradition of naming events that happened before while walking through the places where those events occurred, in effect mindfully traversing a fabled landscape. Australian Aborigines can still point to where their stories tell them they emerged from the dreaming Earth.

We are not so far from this kind of land dreaming that we can't recover a sense of it. All cultures know of sacred places and animated locales. Both the Greeks and Romans believed in a *genius loci* or "spirit of place." An impressive Western land tradition still active here and there tells tales of brownies and sprites, sirens and banshees, naiads and nereids, farthings and fauns. Only with the full onset of the Industrial Revolution did the nature spirits retreat (as Jung pointed out) into the human interior, outwardly suppressed but inwardly active as psychosomatic illnesses and haunting neuroses. These painful returns of the ecopsychologically repressed bedevil a civilization supposedly cleansed of superstition while gazing up at the scientist and the stockbroker for salvation. (One could argue that uncritical belief in "rationality" is the supreme superstition of them all.)

Our experience of place lives on many levels, and so do our ties to the environment. Environmental psychology, launched in the 1940s when social scientist Roger Barker observed that humans are "radically situated," researches the surface connections to our surroundings: amount of sunlight affecting mood, stadium seating influencing crowd noise. Conservation psychology goes somewhat deeper to compare our emotional reactions to those of other primates. Deep ecology goes deeper still, diagnosing the anthropocentric regard of ourselves as masters of nature and offering more benign alternatives.

To begin to understand and appreciate the deepest levels of our relationship with our surroundings, we must make use of an instrument ground finer than those made for measurement. We need myth to illuminate the vibrating threads of symbol and metaphor and affect that keep us in constant but unknowing resonance with what happens to the places we inhabit.

Only myth can answer the question of this chapter: How does my story interlock with the storied presence of the geographical place where I find myself? It must, unless we retreat to the lingering 19th-century view of Earth as a passive heap of raw material and of humans as walking machines—and even then we would find ourselves in yet another story.

Myths of Places

Each place expresses a character or style wider and more complex than its components—including the human ones going into the animate mix. "Place is the greatest thing," said the philosopher Thales, "as it contains all things," from moist to dry to mobile to mindful. Named after the idealistic saint of the natural world, San Francisco exuded a Dionysian aura long before the activists and artists moved in. The very hills rise and fall in swift mood swings surmountable only by cable cars scrounged from the depths of clamorous mines. Structures were going up and coming down in New York City, whose motto is "Excelsior" ("Ever Upward"), before the Americans arrived to level the trees and hills; witness one Dutch governor's complaint that citizens were taking home as souvenirs the stones from a defense bulwark along what is now Wall Street.

To know the character of a place requires some research into the lay of the land, its air and water, its human and prehuman history; what has been and is being built there, its reputation, its lore, the kinds of people who gather there. What makes Paris the City of Light? It always has been, a place of color (photography and the fashion industry started there), vision, fire, art, and science. And yet it also remains a city of splits, from the Seine running through to political polarizations running back to the pre-guillotine legend of St. Dennis carrying his severed head through the city. Each place is unique; an open Oklahoma livestock field feels different than a pasture in Marin even though both spread out in rural regions. To the former belongs a blustery, sky-borne tension as though the land were waiting for something; to the latter, a strange, settled serenity even when the summer sun draws sweat from the backs of cows and ranchers alike.

The inquiry into personal myth continues and expands with the question of which features of a place join up with one's myth. While pursuing my Californian odyssey I returned to San Diego, my place of origin: for me the Ithaca of the Odysseus story. Beyond being my home, San Diego has always been a place of sanctuary. The Kumeyaay people have lived there for millennia. Juan Cabrillo, its first European visitor, called it "a very good port" and sheltered there briefly before moving on up the coast. Long before a border divided California from Mexico, San Diego received its name from the feast day commemorating the defense of a border in Spain.

Something about San Diego exerts a strong sense of protectiveness, from its lamentable militarization by soldiers and missionaries to its natural deflection of vigorous Pacific currents. As with one's personal story, so with the story of a place: when ignored it tends to be acted out unconsciously. How many rising stars have moved to Los Angeles only to end as fallen angels?

A former graduate student of mine has as her myth the priestess of the Oracle. At Delphi, the priestess was known as the Pythonness, originally the servant and spokeswoman of the Great Mother. When my former student moved to Sonoma County, she felt an encompassing sense of homecoming, and no wonder: Sonoma County's resident "god" or mythic structure is Demeter, the mother goddess of earthly wisdom, fertility, and nourishment. The new resident understood her myth to be in alignment with the place's when she reflected on the name of her new street: Pythian Road.

From its study of our deep connections to place, terrapsychology surmises that places too harbor their own version of a personal myth. Prometheus stares out at us from books on Greek myth, but he also lives in Switzerland, mountainous region of perpetual reform and technological animation. *Frankenstein* was written there within eyeshot of what is now a high-energy physics lab. Jung alchemized his brew of depth psychology there. Bisexual Dionysus rumbles through quaking San Francisco dispensing mood swings of ecstasy and enthusiasm. Retirees still move to Florida looking for the Fountain of Youth, and Pele endlessly recreates volcanic Hawaii.

Mozart's Divine Child self might not have done well in introverted Switzerland, but it received some of its nourishment from the theatrics of Vienna. Knowing the character or soul of place well, then, can be a means to knowing some of the further reaches of your myth, including where it wants to restage itself for further elaboration.

The reverse is also true: one's myth can cast light on the nature of a place: a little of the world's soul given illumination by a caring human consciousness.

Personal myth work, which too often stops at the edge of the personal, sometimes attempts to co-opt or absorb the transhuman sphere into the human, as though Mars and Venus had nothing better to do than populate our relationships. To counter this tendency to make it all about ourselves, we invert the question of how a place where we live or lived shows up in one's myth by asking:

What part does my myth play in the story of this place? How is my myth part of its myth?

Personal Myth as Bridge to a Storied World

John Steinbeck grew up in Monterey County, the kingdom of underworldly depth, site of underwater canyons just off the coast, an early civic takeover by Hades-like opportunist David Jacks, and many outlaws and radical artists (some suicidal) gathering around the county. It was here that John Denver crashed like Icarus while attempting to fly his plane over Monterey Bay.

As a knight of literature, Steinbeck's ceaseless local explorations discovered treasures in the underworld: not of money or sardines, but of stories, faces, and landscapes. Many of his characters seem almost to be personifications of nature, like Doc of *Cannery Row*, a man who lived in his instincts. In *To a God Unknown* a farmer lays face down in a field as though making love to it.

Never interested in the self-help or self-exploration genres, Steinbeck emphasized the marginal, the wild, the forgotten, and the nonhuman in his writings. Just as Lancelot's mobile gallantry connected him to the land of Logres he wandered, so did Steinbeck's myth bond him deeply to his place of origin (even Salinas, which he claimed to hate but which recurred in his life and work). In searching and exploring the countryside of Monterey, he did find himself and his calling, for going out, as the naturalist John Muir observed, is really going in. But he also found the inner being of Monterey. In his writing the human realm always reflects and is reflected by the wider world of the nonhuman.

To enlarge the focus even farther:

If personal myths are nested, is it possible that place myths are too? Suppose that Monterey County expresses in turn the depth/underworld component of the psychic reality of California.

What were Steinbeck's knightly obligations toward the Golden State as a whole?

One of the jobs of a knight is to fight injustice. When Steinbeck visited the camps set up for poverty-stricken farmers fleeing from the Dust Bowl during the Depression, the squalid conditions deeply angered him. Even pitching in himself with the manual labor did not make him feel better. It took him two years for his fury to subside to the point where he could sit down and write his well-named novel *The Grapes of Wrath*. It proved far more effective at bringing poverty to public attention than any tabulation of facts and figures. Only after this heartfelt attack on merciless corporate greed did he feel free to leave California for the East Coast.

By contrast the connection between Freud's myth and Vienna's remained unconscious. Freud had been born in Pribor, a Czech town named Freiberg in those days, in a house on Locksmith Lane, an appropriate enough site for the future unlocker of psychological riddles, but by age 4 he lived in Vienna. In a sense he had landed in the right spot. His mythic tragedy fit Vienna's character. With an irregular, roughly circular center unusual for a former Roman garrison town, Vienna was and is an immense stage: to the Babenbergs and the Hapsburgs, Mozart and Strauss, the 1814 Congress that met to redraw the map of Europe after Napoleon was beaten, the showy circular Ringstraße road where Freud used to walk (and which contained the State Opera and the Burgtheater), the Austrian Civil War, and of course the balcony of the Neue Berg from which Hitler ranted in 1938, the year Freud escaped to London. Vienna, future stage to the Vienna International Centre, many balls, opera houses, parks, and gardens, the very first coffee shop anywhere according to local legend, and of course the blue Danube, Europe's second-longest river after the Volga.

Yet Freud never made anything consciously creative out of the resonance between his myth-play and Vienna. He said he disliked the city, and psychoanalysis as he practiced it emphasized the interior world over the exterior. He did compare the psyche to Rome, but for him the comparison remained a fancy. He never followed it up. As a result, the stage itself was interiorized down into the confines of his consulting room, its emotional dramas, and its silent audience of archeological figurines.

As for playwright Jean-Paul Sartre, born wall-eyed in the City of Light, he would never have acknowledged the presence of a personal myth, insisting to the end that meaning is a choice we make and not an elaboration of a template we come in with; yet *how* he lived lit up much more than the vast philosophical tracts he took amphetamines to make himself write. Paris, with its surrealisms, expressionisms, and mobile eyes of flaneurs, lockpicks, artists, and inventors, has never confined itself to witnessing only the pleasantly colorful. Neither did Sartre, who wrote about peering through keyholes and dreading "The Look" of the Other. His Parisian eye roved all over the world as the city's unknowing but effective ambassador. At his life's end, when Simone de Beauvoir asked him how an awkward child had turned into such a cosmopolitan, he replied that even as a boy he recognized that all his favorite writers focused on one subject: the world. This filled him with a lifelong sense of enthusiasm such that when he finally crossed the first frontier, he realized he could cross them all.

In these three lives the personal story not only aligned with a place's story but gave it form, motion, and manifestation: Queen Calafia sending forth her knight errant Steinbeck, Vienna staging Freud's Oedipal replay even without his conscious cooperation, and Paris peering from the outward-gazing eyes of witness-bearing Sartre. Probably all of us, via our personal myth, represent a human expression of our places of origin and those of our current situation. This is where personal myth work can give us a solid sense of belonging to the world, a psychological grounding increasingly absent from industrialized culture. Through our stories, with their twists and trials and tribulations, some of the world and its soul return to life and breath.

Deep Homecoming: Toward a New Myth for Our Time

Surely one of the oddest aspects of "postmodern" life is how few of us feel at home on this planet. Fractured myths jangle down across the face of a fractured world.

As a late result of early Greek rationalism, monotheistic other-worldliness, Cartesian divisiveness, industrialized consumption, and the verbal panegyrics of postmodernism itself, a gap between self and world has opened in human experience. Many of us fall into it through the anguish of belonging nowhere, awash in labels lost among "floating signifiers." So pervasive is this conviction of homelessness that we tend to take it for natural, but historically it represents a jarring abnormality. Primal people feel like part of Earth, but most of us do not anymore.

Because the great regional mythologies that once joined us psychologically to the elements have all undergone a dissipation that cannot be stopped, a truly convincing myth for explaining the world to ourselves would have to be transhuman, transcultural, planetary, and cosmological. Because the psyche is busy eternally mythologizing, it might be worthwhile to keep an eye out for the new myth that could fulfill these conditions, a myth arising not from a particular culture or city or tribe, but shaped by the depths of the collective unconscious. What might this new myth look like? Could our personal myths home in on it somehow?

Joseph Campbell believed that the new myth would involve Earth itself, the ultimate source of every mythology everywhere. Current myths about the planet stand in dire need of updating. Witness how the Earth-as-Mother myth originating in indigenous cultures underwent a tragic appropriation by the dominant industrial growth proponents, who relate to the planet much as a spoiled child relates to Mom, discounting her needs even while sucking the last of the life from her tired frame. Earth as unintelligent resource, as mom to trash, a punisher of humans, or as goddess to worship on bent knee: in none of these mythic constructions do we stand in adult dialog with the planet.

If instead we imagine Earth as living nexus and repository of myth, the old Mother image receives space to dream itself forward, inviting us into conscious conversation with the land, sea, and sky. Coming forth from behind the cultural illusion of their dumbness, the animals, objects, and elements around us can be heard to speak the very same language used by the unconscious: that of symbol, image, and myth. How different the world appears when experienced as animate, and worthy of our love, respect, and protection.

Perhaps the new myth will be welcomed and embraced most ardently by people finished with psychological infancy and adolescence and ready to come home to Earth as mature caretakers and thoughtful listeners and witnesses. Finally understanding how personal stories and place stories and Earth's endlessly circulate, feeding information and perception and emotion and soul into terrestrial networks of an almost infinite complexity. Able at last to appreciate the world up close as well as from the blackness of space. Finally coming of age. In the end, perhaps our personal myths—and perhaps all myths everywhere—float as stories in the planet's imagination. Perhaps if followed far enough, all our myths point us homeward.

For all we know, Earth's own myth spins outward into webs of meaning stretching across a sentient, myth-filled cosmos. Be that as it may, personal myth work ecologized invites us to hold our evolving myths as unfolding plots in the blue-green mind of this floating, dazzling ball of life that deserves our better attentions.

Suggested Reading

Bolen, Jean Shinoda. *Goddess in Everywoman: Powerful Archetypes in Women's Lives.* New York: Harper, 2004.

Bond, D. Stephenson. *Living Myth: Personal Meaning as a Way of Life.* Boston: Shambhala, 1993.

Campbell, Joseph. *Pathways to Bliss: Mythology and Personal Transformation.* Novato: New World Library, 2004.

Cotterell, Arthur. *Dictionary of World Mythology: A Wide-Ranging Guide to Myths, Legends, Deities, and Spirits.* New York: Oxford U Press, 2006.

Downing, Christine. *The Goddess: Mythological Images of the Feminine.* New York: Continuum International Publishing, 1996.

Feinstein, David, and Krippner, Stanley. *The Mythic Path: Discovering the Guiding Stories of Your Past—Creating a Vision for Your Future.* Santa Rosa: Energy Psychology Press/Elite Books, 2006.

Hillman, James. *The Soul's Code: In Search of Character and Calling.* New York: Warner Books, 1996.

Hillman, James. *The Thought of the Heart and the Soul of the World.* Dalls: Spring Publications, 1992.

Hollis, James. *Tracking the Gods: The Place of Myth in Modern Life.* Toronto: Inner City Books, 1995.

Houston, Jean. *A Mythic Life: Learning to Live Our Greater Story.* New York: HarperCollins, 1996.

Jung, C.G., and Jaffe, Aniela, ed. *Memories, Dreams, Reflections.* New York: Vintage, 1989.

Keen, Sam, and Valley-Fox, Anne. *Your Mythic Journey: Finding Meaning in Your Life Through Writing and Storytelling.* Los Angeles: Jeremy P. Tarcher, 1989.

Larsen, Stephen. *The Mythic Imagination: The Quest for Meaning Through Personal Mythology.* Rochester: Inner Traditions International, 1990.

LeGuin, Ursula. *The Telling.* New York: Ace Books, 2000.

Leonard, Scott, and McClure, Michael. *Myth and Knowing: An Introduction to World Mythology.* New York: McGraw-Hill, 2003.

McAdams, Dan. *The Stories We Live By: Personal Myths and the Making of the Self.* New York: The Guilford Press, 1997.

Meade, Michael. *Men and the Water of Life: Initiation and the Tempering of Men.* San Francisco: HarperSanFrancisco, 1994.